HERE'S WHAT THE E

"Every so often a book comes along that not only 'tells it like it is' but shows you what to do about it. Once you start reading, you won't put it down until you're hired. It's the most effective system ever devised!"

—**Carol L. Rhodes, President**
American Employment Association

"Destined to become the bible for job hunters."

—**H. Allen Case, Jr., President**
Arizona Search Consultants Association

"Jeff Allen will show you how to simply get the interview, quickly get the job, and positively ensure your success!"

—**William A. Nilsen, President**
Professional Placement Association

"The author covers more territory, more thoroughly but more concisely, than anyone else has ever done."

—**Marvin Liebowitz, Director**
The Executive Register

"FINALLY! Someone with the experience, the method, and the delivery to get you hired!"

—**Alan R. Schonberg, President**
Management Recruiters International, Inc

"Not only does Allen show you how to quickly get the interview, he shows you how to quickly get the job!"

—**William J. LaPerch, C.P.C., President**
Association of Professional Personnel Agencies

"A savvy writer with a no-nonsense style and a sixth-sense understanding. Readable and doable by anyone."

—**Donald M. Wallach, President**
Maryland Association of Professional Recruitment Consultants

OTHER BOOKS BY JEFFREY G. ALLEN, J.D., C.P.C.

HOW TO TURN
AN INTERVIEW
INTO A JOB

COMPLETELY REVISED AND UPDATED

JEFFREY G. ALLEN, J.D., C.P.C.

A Fireside Book
Published by Simon & Schuster
New York   London   Toronto   Sydney

FIRESIDE
Rockefeller Center
1230 Avenue of the Americas
New York, NY 10020

Copyright © 1983, 2004 by Jeffrey G. Allen, J.D., C.P.C.
This Fireside Edition 2004

FIRESIDE and colophon are registered trademarks
of Simon & Schuster, Inc.

For information regarding special discounts for bulk purchases,
please contact Simon & Schuster Special Sales at 1-800-456-6798
or business@simonandschuster.com.

Designed by Diane Hobbing of Snap-Haus Graphics

Manufactured in the United States of America

10 9 8 7 6 5 4 3 2

Library of Congress Cataloging-in-Publication Data
Allen, Jeffrey, G.
    How to turn an interview into a job / Jeffrey G. Allen.—Rev. and updated ed.
        p.   cm.
    "A Fireside book."
    Includes bibliographical references and index.
    1. Employment interviewing. I. Title.
    HF5549.5.I6A44   2004
    650.14'4—dc22   2003067456

ISBN 0-7432-5349-3

WITH APPRECIATION . . .

To my wife, Bev;
Our daughter, Angel;
Our son ("in-law"), Rudy;
Our grandson, Jonathan; and
Our granddaughter, Gabby.

The greatest family imaginable.

Special thanks to my editor, Amanda Patten, and my assistant, Bea Dinerman.

To all those intelligent, talented,
creative, industrious, energetic
people among the underemployed and unemployed:

May these keys unlock your potential.

CONTENTS

CHAPTER XII
Placement Services: The Job Intelligence Network
Most people don't understand the function of placement services.
Knowing the three basic types and how to use them is indispensable in
switching your career to the fast track. They're the conductors; you're
the engineer.

CHAPTER XIII
Looking While You're Still Employed: Isn't Everybody?
You're measurably more marketable, secure, and confident while still
employed. This is a distinct advantage in being hired *if* you understand
how to keep your options open. Now you'll be shown how.

CHAPTER XIV
P.S. Soon You'll Be Hearing . . .
A few final thoughts about where we've been and where we'll be going.
The results will speak for themselves.

Notes

Bibliography . . . and Why
In the microcosm of finding a job, you can learn important skills to direct
your future. Here is some carefully selected material designed to assist.

Index

INTRODUCTION

I've spent my entire career in the job placement field, and it all comes down to this:

1. A personal interview is *inevitable.*
2. A personal interview is almost *all that counts.*
3. A personal interview is a highly *predictable, controllable event,* with only the places and faces changing.

Everything else—research, phone calls, letters, résumés—is simply backup for that crucial meeting.

Interviewing should be considered as nothing more than packaging yourself for sale. The only difference between selling *yourself* and selling *something else* is that you are both the *goods* and the *salesperson.* In this sense, the interviewing process is unique and your success can be really exciting. It can also be intimidating. You may feel frustrated right now, but this book will give you the confidence you need—and much more.

A successful interview is deceptively simple: the minute, almost imperceptible nuances make the difference. You can control these nuances through specific, proven, easy-to-learn techniques.

Soon you'll discover that exploring your career world and discovering yourself in the process is more interesting, enlightening, and enjoyable than all the psychotherapists' couches, biofeedback mechanisms, and self-help courses you will ever find.

One of the first things I learned in my human resources career was that people don't change, circumstances change. An employee who is eased out of one company for poor work performance goes to another company and becomes a superstar; a person leaves a bad marriage and enters into a good one; a student fails at one school and becomes an honor student at another; the has-been actor wins an Oscar. The opposite also occurs just as often.

Sounds familiar, doesn't it? What is really happening?

Nobody is changing, but different *circumstances* are bringing out different *attributes*. That is why internalizing failure is such an illogical thing to do. (Internalizing success is illogical, too, but at least it gives you self-confidence.)

Forget it—don't fight it. The face in the mirror will always be essentially the same. It's a lot easier to change your circumstances. Life is too short to be slaving away at some dead-end job or knocking on doors. You'll never really know whether you like a job until several weeks after you find the restroom anyway. Plan carefully, get hired, and if you don't like it, go out and *get hired again*! You'll probably increase your salary and end up ahead of the game.

Worried about your work history? Summarize or omit parts of it. Worry about your *life*!

I remember huffing and puffing at some recent college grad like myself, trying to convince him that my new employer should also be his. All the right words were there. He listened patiently. When I caught my breath, he smiled at me with a knowing grin and said, "One fun factory is no better than another, only different."

That was years ago, and I've never forgotten the wisdom of that statement. Today, he'd probably break into a chorus of "Take This Job and Shove It"!

Since then, I've proven my theory that the best person for the job is usually someone who can get hired. I am convinced that the people who interview successfully are the people who are promoted faster, have more self-esteem, and bounce back from the ravages of corporate life faster and higher than anyone else.

I hope that all the hers and shes in this world will understand that the hims and hes in this book are used only for consistency. My thoughts are with you every step of the way.

Before you can turn an interview into a job, you need to *get* the interview. You do this by:

- Preparing a résumé that is clear, concise, and focused.
- Making a critical phone call that will convince the hiring authority to grant you a personal interview.
- Scheduling an interview in a way that will give you the best advantage.

Now, let's get started!

HOW TO TURN
AN INTERVIEW
INTO A JOB

CHAPTER I
Résumé Roulette: How to Play the Game

Literally hundreds of books and articles have been written about résumé preparation. Thousands of companies offer to prepare a résumé for you that they guarantee will get your foot in the door. Unfortunately, the only jobs generated by most of these are for the writers. There is no way to ensure that your résumé will even be read, let alone forwarded!

This has led some people to wonder whether your chances of getting hired are actually better *without* a résumé. The premise is that "if you never do anything, you'll never make a mistake." If Babe Ruth had thought that way, his 1,330 strikeouts would not have occurred. Of course, he would not have hit 714 home runs either. Which are remembered?

To understand why résumés are required, consider the plight of the interviewer. Most interviewers are inundated with a flood of résumés in a variety of shapes, sizes, and colors. Since résumé writing is indeed an art, the old saying "I don't know what's good, I only know what I like" fully applies here. Interviewers also know that résumés reduce telephone time and awkward explanations to candidates. Accepting résumés is nothing more than their way of maintaining their sanity and their job. When blind box advertisements are used, they can even take a lunch break.

Since there is no standard form for writing a résumé, you can understand the fallacy of the words "We have evaluated your background . . ." in the form rejection letters most résumés generate. However, interviewers of this world depend on résumés, so you'd better have one.

A résumé is nothing more than a tool to get your foot in the interviewer's door. (It's not really locked; there's only a chair behind it.) A good one results in an appointment for an interview; a

bad one does not. If buildings were constructed like most résumés, King Kong would have destroyed the world.

Interviewers are so subjective and inconsistent in their responses to résumés that I have described their use as "résumé
roulette." With that understanding, there are a few general rules
that will at least allow you to stay in the game long enough to
make the Deep-Breath Phone Call.

A résumé *should:*

1. BE NO MORE THAN ONE PAGE IN LENGTH

This is frustrating, I know, but an ounce of image is worth a pound
of performance. You simply must resist the temptation to clutter
your résumé with detailed information. (In Chapter X we'll review e-résumé techniques.)

I remember one candidate I was trying to place who insisted on
including on her résumé everything she had ever done from the
time she was a graduate student—over twenty-five years ago! No
one cared. It was ancient history and only drew attention to the
fact that she was a little long in the tooth. She got nowhere until I
convinced her to eliminate everything but her most recent experience and reduce her résumé to a single page. Within a month, she
had a job.

Use general phrases that will incite the interviewer to positive
action—an invitation for an interview. Use phrases like:

- "Developed a series of . . ."
- "Organized several . . ."
- "Was responsible for a number of . . ."
- "Consistently performed . . ."
- "Was promoted to progressively responsible positions
  in . . ."

Try to emphasize actual accomplishments as well, rather than lim-
iting your narrative to generic job requirements that you might, or
might not, have met.

2. BE AT LEAST TEN-POINT SIZE

You can vary the typefaces, boldness, and underlining for interest, but conservative styles will increase the readability of the résumé. My personal preference is Times New Roman.

3. BE PRINTED WITH BLACK INK ON WHITE PAPER

Ivory stock can also be used, and the weight should be at least twenty-four pound. Gray would be acceptable but is often difficult to read and photocopy. Any other ink or paper colors are a mistake. Your relationship with the interviewer is still too fragile, and your résumé may receive attention for a negative reason. Save your individualism for your promotion party.

4. HAVE AT LEAST A ONE-INCH BORDER

This is primarily for aesthetic reasons, but it is common for interviewers to write comments in the margins. If another sheet is required to do so, many will just move on to the next résumé.

5. CONTAIN YOUR NAME, ADDRESS, TELEPHONE NUMBERS, FAX NUMBER, E-MAIL ADDRESS, AND WEBSITE CENTERED AT THE TOP

If any of this information changes, prepare another résumé.

6. CONTAIN INFORMATION ABOUT CREDENTIALS AND CAREER-RELATED AFFILIATIONS

7. SUMMARIZE YOUR EXPERIENCE, WITH THE MOST RECENT EMPLOYER AND POSITION FIRST

Whether you are a generalist or a specialist, this section of your résumé can be written in several different ways. You will find that working backward from the kinds of positions you want will help you to focus on the areas of emphasis. Listing or summarizing similar responsibilities is acceptable, but you must be *concise*. This is known as the "chronological" résumé.

Some authorities advise a "functional" résumé, generalizing your duties, when you have changed jobs more frequently than every two years. Interviewers are accustomed to application forms with chronological sequence. The narrative that a functional résumé recites turns them off. Furthermore, it is almost impossible to draft a generalized résumé without looking as if you're hiding the truth. Use a chronological approach, but combine and omit short-term employment. There is no reason for you to include everything at this stage of the game.

A résumé *should not:*

1. UPDATE OR EMPHASIZE EXPERIENCE IN HAND-WRITING

Updating should be done only through another résumé or an attached application neatly typed in advance. Underlining or other emphasizing should either be done at the time the résumé is prepared or not at all. Since the résumé is *you* at this point, make sure it has class.

2. CONTAIN INFORMATION ON REFERENCES

Instead, you should state the following: "Personal and professional references are available. They will be furnished upon request." References are too precious to annoy, and you want to be able to contact them *first*. This rule may be broken if you are relying on a highly motivated internal referral.

3. STATE A SALARY

This includes the amount you received in former positions and that which is your requirement. At the early stages, it is a no-win gamble: it invariably will be too high or too low. Besides, your value to someone else or even to yourself is irrelevant. This will become more evident when you read Chapter VII, on salary negotiation.

Whenever possible, send your résumé directly to the hiring authority rather than to the human resources department, where you can get lost in the shuffle. When the human resources department is the only option, your résumé *should not:*

1. STATE YOUR OBJECTIVE

That is, unless you know the job being offered and you don't care about being considered for anything else. This is also the problem with introductory letters. You are just foreclosing your options. You objective is getting an *interview*!

2. BE ACCOMPANIED BY A COVER LETTER

A cover letter to an unidentified target can be counterproductive, pointing you away from the job opening. Unless you *really* know something about the job, or want to name the source of your referral, resist the temptation. Overworked human resources people will think of it as just one more piece of paper to shuffle.

However, if you are aiming at a departmental *decision maker,* an eye-catching cover letter has exactly the opposite effect! It directs you right where you want to be.

A well-written cover letter is crucial in this case: it serves to introduce you and spark a decision maker's interest. If you've done your homework, here's a place to use it. Your letter should meet a prospective employer on his own turf. Start with a comment or two on the company—perhaps concerning recent developments you have read or heard about within the field—and how your work experience might fit in. Close by suggesting your ultimate goal: an interview.

Your homework should include a phone call to the company to find out the correct spelling of the executive's name, his exact title, the full name of the company, and other details. There is no greater turn-off to a prospective employer than having his name or his company's name misspelled.

Like a résumé, a cover letter should be neatly typed—not in italic or other "handwriting" typefaces—on white paper (preferably your personal business stationery with your name, address, telephone numbers, fax number, e-mail address, and website conservatively imprinted).

Your résumé will be the goods, but the letter is the package.

Therefore, it must reflect quality. We are motivating now, not educating.

The following three items are optional but worth considering. A résumé *may:*

1. CONTAIN A PHOTOGRAPH

Consideration of your face in the hiring process violates federal, state, and local equal employment opportunity laws, except under very limited circumstances. Inclusion of a photograph is therefore a matter of concern to employers, and only a matter of strategy to you. My *personal* opinion is that you shouldn't; my *personnel* opinion is that you shouldn't; but my *legal* opinion is that you can. Whether you should is best left to your judgment. But keep in mind that professional interviewers in some companies will not forward a résumé with a photograph attached.

Also bear in mind that your photograph might inadvertently trigger a negative reaction. A colleague of mine once got a résumé from a woman who enclosed a photograph. She looked exactly like his ex-wife. He tossed her résumé in the wastebasket without even bothering to talk to her. Maybe he did this not because he was in the midst of a vicious divorce but because she wasn't qualified. Who knows? But why take a chance?

2. CONTAIN INFORMATION THAT RELATES TO SEX, HEIGHT, WEIGHT, HEALTH, MARITAL STATUS, AGE, RACE, RELIGION, PLACE OF BIRTH, OR CITIZENSHIP

As with a photograph, these allow the interviewer or supervisor to decide your fate based upon irrelevant and illegal criteria. You run the risk of a recipient automatically discriminating against you on the basis of this information.

If you want to know the effect of these factors, you can try calling the employer anonymously. Ask a few general questions about its commitment to affirmative action without arousing suspicion. While the information you receive may not be accurate, you will at least have some indication of what to expect. Affirmative action statements in advertisements are meaningless, since they are designed for public and government consumption.

3. USE AN ATTENTION-GETTING GIMMICK

Why not reduce and insert your résumé into a fortune cookie? An applicant sent me a package like that once. It was a real grabber. I always felt that sending him "No Interest Letter No. 2" was not quite enough. If you happen to see a half-eaten pita bread stuffed with printed paper on some interviewer's desk as you search for a job, this applicant's probably still on the loose.

Your approach should be just to get your foot in the interviewer's door as inconspicuously as possible. Attention? You'll get attention! The rest of you is about to enter. It's time for the Deep-Breath Phone Call.

CHAPTER II

The Deep-Breath Phone Call: "I'll Call You!"

If you have ever waited around for a response to the old "send me a résumé" or "submit an application" routine, you need no further convincing that the game just switched from roulette to poker . . . and you'd better know the rules.

Authorities term the internalizing of too many negative responses "rejection shock." This insidious disease has attacked millions and is now a national epidemic. Heart palpitations when talking with prospective employers are the major symptom, if its victims get that far. But don't worry—here is the cure. Watch out for the side effect: *acceptance* shock!

In his classic book *Power! How to Get It, How to Use It,* Michael Korda states: "The person who receives a telephone call is always in an inferior position of power to the person who placed it."[1]

It is this phenomenon, coupled with your anxiety about being hired, that can push your foot out of the interviewer's door while waiting for a call. There is only one way to break the "don't call us, we'll call you" syndrome: *Take a deep breath and call the interviewer!*

I know you will be thinking that the interviewer will be angry at you, and you will therefore not be hired. It's like calling your first blind date. But the reality is that you're just replaying old memories. In fact, the average interviewer is so busy trying to place job orders, run advertisements, review résumés, arrange for interviews, interview, verify employment data, check references, rationalize why the position hasn't been filled, and justify exceeding the hiring budget, that there is no *time* to be angry.

As Maxwell Maltz noted in his classic *Psycho-Cybernetics:*

A human being always acts and feels and performs in accordance with what he imagines to be true about himself and his environment. This is a basic and fundamental law of mind. It is the way we are built.[2]

When you call is extremely important, because you want your initial conversation with the interviewer to be at a time when he will be most receptive and when you are fully prepared. Statistically, this should be any Tuesday through Friday between 9:00 A.M. and 11:00 A.M.

Mondays are unpredictable and should be avoided, because the interviewer's nervous system will still be stabilizing from the weekend, he might be nursing a hangover (an occupational disease among people who are hiring), new hires are being processed, the employer may be deluged with e-mails and telephone calls from advertisements in the Sunday paper, and staff meetings are more likely.

Friday mornings are particularly opportune, because employees are terminating, and important decisions are not made on Fridays. This means that the interviewer may learn for the first time that a requisition exists and will defer discussing the position with you by arranging an interview. Friday afternoons are even worse than Monday mornings, because "exit interviews" are generally conducted. These are the "back end" of a human resources position, and the further away you are, the better.

There are an infinite number of variables in phone conversations, and you might be calling a supervisor directly. However, the illustration that follows will give you an idea of how to position yourself. The words may vary, but your *attitude* shouldn't.

Now . . . sitting comfortably at your desk . . . take a deep breath . . . exhale slowly . . . and place the call:

RECEPTIONIST:	Good morning, Company X.
YOU:	Hi. Ms. (*last name*), please This is (*first name*) (*last name*) calling.
RECEPTIONIST:	May I tell her what this is regarding?
YOU:	(*First name*) asked me for background information regarding the (*title*) position.
RECEPTIONIST:	Have you sent us a résumé?

YOU:	Yes, and I need to fill her in on a couple of points.
RECEPTIONIST:	Just a moment, please. I'll ring. . . . Sorry, the line is busy. Can I take your number?
YOU:	No, I'm sorry . . . I'll be out of the office. I'd better wait.
RECEPTIONIST:	It might be a while.
YOU:	I'll wait, thanks.
RECEPTIONIST:	I can ring now.
INTERVIEWER:	(*First name*) (*last name*).
YOU:	Hi, Ms. (*last name*). This is (*first name*) (*last name*). I've been hoping to hear from you to discuss the (*title*) position.
INTERVIEWER:	I'm sorry, we've been just deluged with responses. You're still being considered and we hope to let you know within a week or so.
YOU:	I know how hectic things must be. I'm under a bit of pressure myself, and it looks like I'll have to make a decision soon. The (*title*) position sounds like a great opportunity, and I'd really like to discuss it personally as soon as possible.
INTERVIEWER:	Hang on a minute . . . Oh, here's your résumé. . . . When did you leave your last employer?
YOU:	I'm sorry, but I'm just about to leave for an appointment. I'd really like to meet you soon. How about tomorrow morning at 8:00?
INTERVIEWER:	I can see you at 9:30.
YOU:	I'll rearrange my schedule. I'm looking forward to meeting you!
INTERVIEWER:	Thank you. See you then.
YOU:	Good-bye.
INTERVIEWER:	Good-bye.

You have been direct, time-conscious, businesslike, and *affirmative.* You have played out your poker hand in a measured way, and have gathered a few chips. The trick is to get the interviewer on the phone, and you off the phone and into her office.

Although I have represented the interviewer as being in the human resources department rather than in the department where you will actually be working, the principles are exactly the same. Generally, the higher the job, the higher the level of the person you can safely contact. The risk is that you will alienate the human resources department, so proceed with caution. Interviewers in human resources screen rather than hire. Your ultimate goal is to reach the decision maker!

The Internet age has also produced the online interview. The preliminary steps haven't changed. You answer a job announcement and forward your résumé. If the company is interested, it might do an initial telephone interview. If you pass this hurdle, a personal interview is arranged. Today, an additional step is often inserted before the phone interview in the form of one or more e-mail messages between a jobseeker and the hiring authority. These are designed to give an employer an idea of the jobseeker's appropriateness for the position. These e-mail messages are really part of the interview process. The process may not be this formal. Often, it is an informal information exchange that happens when e-mail is used.

Once a simple device that let people communicate with one another over long distances, the telephone has become increasingly sophisticated, and many new features can help you in your job search. These include **cell phones, pagers, answering machines, voice mail, and call waiting.** Take advantage of these innovations and include the phone in your job search arsenal.

The telephone, too, can have many pitfalls. Here are some tips on using the telephone in your job search.

Never use the phone where you currently work, not even if you make your calls after hours and from the privacy of your own office. You might be caught, and you don't want your return phone calls intercepted by someone else in the office. It raises a red flag and it's just too dangerous. It also gives your potential employer the wrong message. If you're willing to use the facilities of your current boss surreptitiously, you might do the same to him in the future.

Use your home phone number as your contact point. If you have a family and aren't the only person in your house using this number, get a second line and use it as the dedicated phone for your job search. There's nothing worse than having a prospective employer return your call and have the phone answered by someone who is obviously your mother, your wife, or your two-year-old. It's unprofessional and immediately conveys the wrong impression. The extra expense is worth it, and you can always cancel this second line once you've found a job.

Get a good answering machine or voice mail that lets you pick up messages from outside the house and *leave a brief, professional-sounding message. "Hello, this is John Jones. I'm not available at this time. Please leave your name, number, and the time you called, and I'll get back to you shortly."* It's short, it's sweet, and it's to the point. *Here's another tip:* Even if you're home when the phone rings, don't answer it. Let your answering machine respond. This gives you time to organize your thoughts, review your information, and get ready to have your conversation before you actually return the call. Be prompt in returning your calls, but don't deprive yourself of the time you need to put yourself in the right frame of mind. Letting your answering machine do the work instead of picking up the phone yourself also counters the impression that you're sitting at home unemployed, desperately waiting for the phone to ring with a job offer.

Here are some things *not* to do.

Don't use a cell phone for making your calls. They can be unpredictable, unclear, and frustrating for both you and the person you're talking to.

Don't use a speaker phone. The echo can be very distracting. The person on the other end of the line never knows if someone else in the room is privy to the conversation, which makes that person hesitant to speak freely. Speaker phones also convey the impression that you're doing several things at once and don't think your conversation is important enough to warrant your full attention.

Don't use call waiting. The *click-click* sound of a call coming in while you're on the phone interrupts your conversation in a most destructive way. If you ignore the signal and keep talking, it's distracting. If you put your current call on hold and see who's on the other line, it disrupts the dialogue and gives the person you've been talking to the sense that the incoming call is more important to you than he is.

Once the hiring authority has agreed to an interview, you have to do one more thing before you can strut your stuff. You have to *schedule* the interview.

CHAPTER III

How to Schedule Interviews: Timing Is Everything (Almost)

There is a tendency, particularly when you have not been eating regularly, to set up interviews in a random manner. The result is a wide variance in your metabolic rate, attention span, and response time.

If you were laid off or fired from your last job, a measured approach to interview scheduling is the only way to get you emotionally back on track. It is a psychological fact that physical activity is the best cure for depression. Make interviewing your job until a better one comes along.

The winners in sports and almost every other human endeavor know that consistency is what gives them the edge. You are exercising your interviewing muscles and are jogging . . . not running . . . not walking. If you are out of work, set your goal at one interview around 9:00 A.M. and one interview around 2:00 P.M. Neither should last more than two hours.

Interviews can be much shorter. A very short interview is a bad sign. It means you've said or done something that turned the interviewer off. It's your job to extend it and use the added time to your advantage.

Use a calendar with room for daily entries, and set up appointments compulsively: two a day. Soon, you'll have rhythm. It will do wonders for your self-confidence.

As discussed in Chapter II, Friday afternoons are often a poor time to inquire about your résumé because exit interviews are often conducted. But if you *can* arrange an interview, do so.

Another advantage of consistent scheduling is that you will become accustomed to your own reactions when your body chemistry is in the same balance. This will give you an internal predictability and stabilize your nervous system. After a few days, you will find your self-confidence rising.

The two-hour time limit is critical for two reasons:

1. You want it to appear as though you have another commitment. If you don't, make one. People always want what they can't have, and you're starting to run out of gas anyway.

2. Avoid eating a meal with someone during the hiring process. There is so much that can go wrong in terms of personal mannerisms, offhand remarks, eating or drinking habits, and etiquette, that the "businessman's special" can be *you*! For higher-level positions, this may be unavoidable, so attempt to act discreetly. If it is merely an invitation and not a requirement, graciously decline. You don't want to sacrifice a job for a meal.

We're now ready for the almighty interview. The rest is easy.

CHAPTER IV

The Irresistible Interview: Twelve Steps to the Offer

If résumé contact is roulette and telephone contact is poker, interview contact is tennis. To the extent that you understand the difference, you will transform interviews into offers.

Interviewing and tennis do not depend upon the chance of roulette or the nerves of poker. Instead, they depend upon approach, practice, and hundreds of conditioned responses. This is why actual experience is so critical to developing your skills at winning, regardless of the court (office) or your opponent (interviewer). You can even make mistakes, as long as there are not too many. Nice to know.

Some novices believe interviewing is a frightening and uncertain mystery. Others are convinced "qualifications" for the "position" are somehow being evaluated. Ask the next person you see, and you will probably get another view. These and other misconceptions arise because the interview is really too complex to be analyzed in its totality.

The development of irresistible interviewing depends upon identifying and controlling twelve chronological steps.

Hang on, Company X, *we're coming through*!

1. FAMILIARIZE YOURSELF WITH THE EMPLOYER.

Developing a profile of each employer you visit not only dramatically increases your ability to impress the interviewer but is an important first step in reducing your fear of the unknown. Doing your homework in this area can acquaint you with the number of employees, business locations, products, sales, profits, future plans, and a variety of other elements that make up the personality of any business. As you become adept at doing your homework for each employer, you will find that you can take almost 95 percent of the mystery out of interviewing. From the very beginning, your confidence will show.

Our interviewing approach is aimed directly at the *interviewer.* It doesn't matter if you're applying for a management position or an entry-level job. Either way, it works!

There are two ways to find out about the employer:

The formal (coward's) way. Your local public library provides a wealth of information on almost all publicly held and many privately held companies. Spend a few hours in the reference section. The Internet is another excellent resource. See Chapter X for more on this.

Corporate profiles can be found using the following websites:

COMPANY RESEARCH SITES

Big Book	(bigbook.com)
Biz Web	(bizweb.com)
Business Week	(businessweek.com/search.htm)
Business Wire	(businesswire.com)
Companies Online	(companiesonline.com)
Company Web Pages	(interpiznet.com/hunt/companies)
Edgar	(sec.gov/edgarhp.htm)
Fortune	(fortune.com)
Hoovers	(hoovers.com)
Job Options	(joboptions.com)
Job Safari	(jobsafari.com)
Morningstar	(morningstar.com)
PR Newswire	(prnewswire.com)
Vault	(vault.com)
Wet Feet	(wetfeet.com)

Since so much information is available, you may be tempted to memorize a lot of statistics about the employer. Don't! Just look up the information, write down a few items of interest, and move

on to the next employer fortunate enough to have you available
for an interview. Review your notes periodically, simply to store
the information in your brain. It will be ready for use at the appropriate time without any further conscious thought.

The informal (hero's) way. After the first week of scheduling
two interviews a day, you will start to become an "Interviewaholic." You may even have received some job offers. If you are still
discovering your worth, or if you are an outgoing person anyway,
the fastest, most enjoyable, and most effective way to learn about
the personality of the employer is by a telephone call. In small organizations, it may be the *only* way, so be prepared to do so.

No deep breath required here. Just call the sales department,
marketing department, public relations department, or receptionist, and state the purpose of your call. Then plan on doing a lot of
listening. People love to talk about their jobs and their companies.
At some point along the line, you'll probably be the one to terminate the conversation.

Here's an added bonus: If you play your cards right, you may
end up with an *internal referral!* There is no more potent entry
into any company, since the interviewer will feel obligated to act
upon the referral and go forward with an interview. If you look at
all good, he'll be inclined to give you the benefit of the doubt.
Otherwise, he'll be faced with more than one embarrassing eleva-
tor ride if he rejected you for the position.

I'll bet you didn't realize you had friends in such high and low
places. Your appreciation should be expressed by a note and return
telephone call after the interview. If this seems a little unorthodox,
wait until you see the *rest* of our serves to the interviewer!

2. DRESS PROPERLY.

John Molloy, in his landmark book *Dress for Success,* starts with
a premise that more than two million people have already bought:

> Those of you who are . . . saying that fashion is an art form
> and not a science are making the same kind of statement as
> the eighteenth-century doctors who continued to bleed peo-
> ple. I do not contend that fashion is an absolute science, but

I know that conscious and unconscious attitudes toward dress can be measured and that this measurement will aid men in making valid judgements about the way they dress.[3]

The reactions to styles, colors, and combinations of clothing are highly predictable. So are the tastes of human resources professionals. A carefully chosen interviewing "uniform" on a well-groomed applicant maximizes a favorable response.

The interviewing uniform for men

This is the easiest part, because there is really only one way for any man to dress for almost any employment interview.
Navy blue three-piece suit. Wool and wool blends look better and last longer. Solid colors or subdued stripes are preferred. Gray may be worn, but Brooks Brothers has never been able to manufacture natural-shoulder navy blue suits fast enough to meet the demand. Shiny fabrics should be avoided, and no religious, fraternal, or service pins should be worn.
White long-sleeved dress shirt. Laundered and starched commercially! Your interviewer won't wear a monogram, and, therefore, you shouldn't. Collar style should be current, and if French cuffs are worn, cuff links should also not reflect any religious, fraternal, or service affiliation. They should be the same color as your watch, and neither should be larger than necessary.
Dark blue striped tie. A contrasting color is acceptable, but the predominant color should be the same as your suit. Silk or other thin fabrics are recommended.
Black dress shoes. Almost any style is acceptable, as long as they can be polished well, and are.
Since the uniform for men doesn't vary for most jobs, you should have at least two or three conservative suits and ties you can use for multiple interviews.
These four items comprise the all-American look in the fashion industry. Almost every consultant agrees on its positive effect. I appeared on a radio talk show with a famous designer who commented that when it comes to business wear, "men's fashions" is really a contradiction in terms. There are almost no trends.

The interviewing uniform for women

There is far more flexibility in clothing for women. A dress or suit should be worn, preferably in subdued colors and fabrics. The following should be avoided:

Low V-necks
High hemlines
Jewelry reflecting any religious or organizational affiliation
Gaudy fashion jewelry
Oversize handbags
Excessive makeup
Heavy perfume
Pants are okay (no jeans!), but they should be worn only
with a matching jacket.

There is increasing evidence that extremely attractive women are not hired as readily by men *or* women. Therefore, if you've got it, don't flaunt it.

If you're budget-minded, the proliferation of discount, wholesale, and factory-direct clothing outlets permits you to acquire an interviewing uniform without taking out a bank loan. Comparison shopping can save you a fortune, and women especially are likely to find famous-maker clothes with different (or no) labels.

Remember, interviewers will look at your clothes, but they won't see the labels.

If you require extensive alterations on ready-to-wear clothes, you might check out custom tailors. The prices are often only slightly higher, but the look is *great*!

For both men and women, regardless of the position, an attaché case is an excellent accessory. It looks businesslike and identifies you with the interviewer. Dark brown is more popular, but I prefer black for men, since it matches the shoes. The case should be wide enough to store breath spray, deodorant, cologne, nonsmoking tablets (if necessary), a comb or brush, a gold pen with black ink, business cards, a legal pad (the kind lawyers use to intimidate), and six extra copies of your résumé. Borrow the case if you must, but don't use one with somebody else's initials on it.

The exceptions that prove the rule of conservative dress are few and far between: highly creative art and entertainment jobs are where they are found. However, looking the part of the job you hope to find is far less powerful than looking the part of the person who will hire you for it. Yes, you can dress differently . . . if you know what a supervisor in a creative department will be wearing.

Even in fad and fashion industries, human resources professionals tend to be conservative. Their decisions are often made in groups, and interview success will vary to the extent that you stray from middle-class and middle-management values in their structured world. You can always dress down a little when you arrive. You can't dress up.

3. ARRIVE ALONE.

You may think that your companion is an asset to bring. You may think that you need moral support. You may think it doesn't matter. You may not even think about it at all. You should.

Nothing good can come from bringing someone with you. The prejudices of the interviewer are already a problem, and you will appear unprofessional at best.

I could see one candidate from my door as she sat in the waiting room. She had brought her boyfriend with her, and they sat there holding hands and nuzzling each other and whispering in each other's ears. She was a qualified candidate, but I must admit that this display tainted my overall impression of her.

Until you are hired, you and your spouse or companion should also avoid any after-hours social gatherings where your interviewer might be present.

We are invoking an absolute rule: HE TRAVELS FASTEST WHO TRAVELS ALONE.

You violate it at your peril.

4. ARRIVE ON TIME.

Any receptionist in America will tell you that appointment punctuality follows a standard bell-shaped curve: one-third of the visitors will be early, one-third will be on time, and one-third will be late. Furthermore, if you are not sensitized to the problem, *you*

will be on time for only one out of every three interviews.
Let's consider why punctuality is so critical:

If you arrive too early

Arriving early is not the same as arriving on time. Students at motivational and sales seminars are indoctrinated with the idea that being early is somehow better. I can see the point if it's "open seating"
(and therefore "open season") at the seminar, but otherwise this is a
serious mistake. When it comes to interviewing, only fools rush in.

Those time-conscious important individuals who do enter
through the human resources department don't sit around in employment lobbies filling out applications. Instead, they arrive outside the building approximately a half hour early and survey the
premises to get their bearings. They review their notes, initiate
conversations, read bulletin boards for information, and are
friendly to those they meet. They may eat a light snack and perhaps drink a cup or two of coffee.

Incidentally, I recommend coffee highly as insurance to keep
you on your toes during the interview and improve your attentiveness and attitude. Coffee has a predictable, harmless, positive effect for interviewing purposes. Caffeine is more than just a
stimulant: it is an antidepressant and has been proven to cause the
neurons in the brain cells to fire faster. This means you will store
and retrieve information more rapidly. That is why many organizations provide it to employees without charge.

If coffee makes you jumpy and irritable, or if you have a history of digestive or blood pressure problems, try regular tea instead. It's less powerful but has fewer side effects.

Eating a light snack is mentioned not only to avoid an attack of
the "munchies," but also because you don't want your blood sugar
level to drop abruptly. This can make you irritable, and prone to
fatigue. The best snacks are those convenient packages of cracker
sandwiches with cheese or peanut butter, since the proportions of
starch, protein, and bulk are just right. The worst snacks are fruit
and candy, since they will accelerate the drop in your blood sugar
level.

Back to our early birds: They find the restroom and "rest,"
check themselves out in the mirror, freshen up; and, promptly,

eyes forward, chin up, shoulders back, stomach in, feet straight, confidently, self-assured, poised, in they march, over to the receptionist, introduce themselves politely and state whom they are there to see. Then they give the receptionist the neatly typed application they received a few days earlier.

I know you were thinking about all of these things anyway, so here's an even more important reason not to arrive too early: it puts pressure on the interviewer. Interviewers don't like to be pressured any more than they are. They have ways of dealing with you. It also puts pressure on you by giving you too much time to think and panic.

If you arrive too late

Arriving too late means you're not time-conscious. It also means you're not considerate.

Interviewers are human. They'll understand if you telephone ahead to reschedule the appointment because of unforeseen traffic congestion (winning applicants are never lost), a hold-up in progress, or any of your other garden-variety excuses. However, if you don't think fast, you'll be subject to the following unwritten rule, which I have just written: INTERVIEWERS WHO WAIT DON'T SCREAM, THEY SCREEN.

As I said, they have ways of dealing with you. Leave as unceremoniously as you arrived, wait six months, and start reading at Chapter I.

The more important reason to avoid being late is that you'll have to start out the interview with an apology. This directly feeds into the subordinate role of an applicant and automatically turns your first serve into a fault. Do your apologizing, if at all, by telephone, before you set foot at the baseline.

5. THE MAGIC FOUR HELLO.

The initial greeting with the interviewer is particularly critical, since this is when the stereotype seeds are planted. Professional interviewers unconsciously form rigid first impressions owing to the large volume of contacts they make, the "fire-fighting" nature of their duties, and the arbitrary and inconsistent requirements imposed by law and management. Stereotyping, like insisting on résumés, becomes a matter of survival.

If this seems an overstatement, in companies with fewer than five hundred employees, it is not unusual to have wage and salary, insurance, employee benefits, labor relations, affirmative action, management development, security, medical, training, safety, mail, telephone operations, plant maintenance, food service, company functions, civic activities, and a variety of other administrative duties performed by the same person who just walked out to talk to you about the same position everyone else in the lobby is applying for. Expediency and stereotyping are the order of the day, and the greeting may be your first and only chance to make a good impression before the interruptions start.

The Magic Four Hello consists of the following simultaneous acts:

1. A smile.
2. Direct eye contact.
3. The words, "Hi, I'm (*first name*) (*last name*). It's a pleasure meeting you."
4. A firm but gentle handshake.

As before, practice makes perfect in coordinating these four elements. A proper handshake is often the hardest to master.

Enthusiasm in the handshake properly sets the tempo of the interview. However, the law of averages we discussed with regard to arriving on time also applies here: experienced interviewers know that they will be subjected to "bone crusher" handshakes approximately one-third of the time. Another third will be "dead fish" handshakes. One type is painful, the other is cold, but both create a negative impression. If you have either of these problems, practice shaking hands with your friends. They may get tired of you, but your career may depend on it.

Down the shelf from *Power!* and *Dress for Success* is another classic book entitled *Contact: The First Four Minutes,* by Leonard Zunin. It emphasizes the importance of first impressions and contains an entire chapter on the importance of the handshake.

A moist palm may merely show someone is nervous, a symbol which automatically eliminates any job applicant at at least one large company of which I am aware. Its personnel director once told me that regardless of the qualifications of a man he interviews, "if his handshake is weak and clammy, he's out." Such reaction to body language is probably far more prevalent than we realize, as others assume many things about our glance, stance, or advance.

We shake hands thousands of times in a lifetime, and it is unfortunate that most of us get little or no feedback on whether or not others like or dislike our handshake.[4]

Dr. Zunin actually conducts handshake workshops. The participants receive ratings from others far different from their own. Make sure yours is above average.

6. AVOID ASSUMING A SUBORDINATE ROLE.

If you could videotape your way through the maze you followed after the Magic Four Hello, you would find at least a hundred different cues that could influence the outcome of the interview. Examples are the color scheme, the temperature, the pictures on the walls, a glance at the employees, and an overheard remark.

Even the liveliest child is quiet in a new environment. Being afraid, dependent upon factors beyond your control, and under close scrutiny puts you in a subordinate role.

Some applicants are aware of this danger and overcompensate by trying to write the script for the interview in advance. This gives them a plastic, unnatural image that gets them nothing except more dress rehearsals.

Physical positioning is especially important. I have an uncle who is extremely successful, and he made it a point to arrange his office in such a way that his desk was always at a higher level than the rest of the room, putting his visitors at a lower level than himself and forcing them to look up at him. This can have a potent psychological impact. If this happens to you, don't fall into the trap and assume a subordinate mind-set.

The "instant replay" effect of unsuccessful interviews is psychologically devastating and turns them into self-fulfilling prophecies for the future. In *Psycho-Cybernetics,* Dr. Maltz recalls how a similar problem affected one of his patients.

His fear and nervousness were overcome in just one coun-
seling session, during which I asked him: . . . "Would you go
into a man's office with your hand out like a beggar and beg
for a dime for a cup of coffee?"

"Certainly not."

"Can't you see that you are doing essentially the same
thing, when you go in overly concerned with whether or not
he will approve of you?"

Thank you, Dr. Maltz! And thank you also for:

Many of us unconsciously and unwittingly, by holding negative attitudes and habitually picturing failure to ourselves in
our imagination, set up goals of failure.[5]

It all comes down to the basic human needs for security, safety,
and acceptance. The more you analyze them, the more compli-
cated they become.

Fortunately, there is a simple, fail-safe device you can use to
avoid assuming a subordinate role: COMPLIMENT THE INTER-
VIEWER ON SOMETHING IN HIS OFFICE, AND ASK ADMIRINGLY
ABOUT IT. Then plan to do a lot of listening. You will notice a stat-
uette of a hula dancer from Maui, or some equally interesting arti-
fact. The more the interviewer talks, the more you are learning.
And not about Maui, either.

7. ALIGN WITH THE INTERVIEWER.

WILL ROGERS: I never met a man I didn't like.
JEFF ALLEN: Neither did I. That's why I never saw a job
                I couldn't get.

Many people have the intuitive ability to obtain any job they
want, because somewhere along the line they discovered that *lik-
ing the interviewer* dramatically invokes a powerful law of human
motivation: PEOPLE LIKE PEOPLE WHO LIKE THEM.

A job interview is not the place to demonstrate your individual-
ity. In *Power!,* Korda concludes a chapter entitled "Nice Guys
Finish First" by stating:

A great deal can be gained by simply learning to smile, an exercise which is not all that easy for many people to perform. The person who wants to use power must learn to control his facial muscles, his temper and himself, and avoid taking "tough stands" where they aren't necessary. Flexibility and cheerfulness are better weapons than brute force, and if used properly have the advantage of making your rivals forget that you're a competitor for power.[6]

During my first day on the job as an interviewer, I was warned to avoid the "halo effect." Seventeen years later, I am still no closer to explaining how this can be done. The halo effect simply means that when you identify with a candidate, he can do no wrong. If you know how to make this psychological fact work for you, you can zap any interviewer into submission within seconds.

Pacing is another accepted psychological technique that has been developed to increase rapport with others. It stems from an even more powerful law of human motivation: WE LIKE PEOPLE WHO ARE LIKE OURSELVES. If you think about it, our entire hiring process is guided by this law. So is almost every other human decision we make about others, including voting, selection of spouses and friends, television and radio choices, product purchases, etc. For our highly specialized purpose, it means *aligning* yourself with the overworked and underpaid interviewer, then leading (steering) him almost imperceptibly, but irresistibly, into extending an offer.

I use pacing all the time in court proceedings, administrative hearings, negotiations, and other high-roll situations. You can win the ones you thought were lost if you know how to do it properly. Pacing has been so effective in influencing hiring authorities, many companies have incorporated these techniques into their standard operating procedures. It even works over the telephone and can be used during the Deep-Breath Phone Call. You simply *must* have a common ground before you can move toward a mutual goal.

How are you going to do it? Here we go:

A. Learn job-related employment and company buzzwords.

Buzzwords are the "insider" language that has developed in every subculture since Adam talked to Eve. Their primary use in pacing is to lock in the alignment with the interviewer. Once you are inside his head, you can lead him effectively. Using them also gives him the impression that you have a working knowledge of how the system works. It makes you look professional. These buzzwords are an indispensable part of a successful interviewing strategy.

If you are already working in the field, you should be able to use job-related buzzwords fluently. Every occupation has them, and you should know what they are. Company buzzwords can be learned by using the methods described earlier for familiarizing yourself with the employer. The following list of employment buzzwords and definitions should get you started.

Acceptance. The easiest response to any job offer. "When do I start?" are the words used.

Affirmative action: Programs designed to encourage the hiring of minorities and women through outreach activities and preferential treatment given in hiring members of these groups.

Available labor pool. What you are walking on, rather than swimming in.

Contact information. Your name, address, telephone numbers, fax number, e-mail address, and website.

Curriculum vitae. The résumé of a nuclear physicist.

Discrimination: Treating an employee differently because of age, sex, race, or ethnicity.

Downsizing: A reduction in the workforce that a company must do in order to meet its financial goals and stay competitive.

Exit interview. The termination debriefing, when you should say nice things about your former boss and everyone else.

Fired. Something you should avoid being. If it occurs, discuss a possible resignation with the firing authority.

Internal referral. Someone working for your potential employer who will act as your public relations representative.

Involuntary termination. One of two ways employment is severed. Generally refers to layoffs and termination for cause. The latter is the same as being fired and requires the same corrective action.

Job comparability. The similarity between what you have done and what the employer is considering for you to do. Even if they appear totally different, 90 percent or more of every job is comparable. It's all in the eye of the beholder.

Job congruence. The extent to which the job being offered conforms to what you want to do. Your attitude should be that they are identical, or congruent.

Job description. An internal list of the duties of a particular position. Looks good on paper, but tells you more about the individual who wrote it than about the job.

Job order. Authorization to a placement service containing a summary of the position, salary range, and type of individual sought. Generally bears no similarity to the person eventually hired.

Job rotation. A system whereby some employers designate certain employees to rotate jobs, so each learns the functions of a certain activity.

Labor grade. A device used in wage and salary administration to rank jobs in order of their value and compensation.

New hire. What you will be on your first day at Company X.

Offer. Something you receive as a result of packaging and selling yourself properly. Often occurs at the time of the first interview after following the techniques in *How to Turn an Interview into a Job.*

Opportunity. The employer has a great one for you.

Personal references. Those dependent on you for support or who owe you money.

Professional references. Former instructors, supervisors, coworkers, and other people familiar with your academic or occupational history and qualifications.

Qualifications. Combination of "*qualit*y," "*fi*t," and "*occupation.*" You have them.

Quotas. A company's stated goal in terms of the minimum number of minorities and women it plans to hire.

Rate range. A device used in wage and salary administration to determine the lowest and highest amount that will be paid for a specific job. A critical consideration for incumbents in any position.

Requisition ("rec"). The form that is initiated by a supervisor to obtain approval for hiring. Once the approval cycle is completed, it becomes an open requisition ("open rec").

Résumé. Something with your contact information, room for notes, job history, and enough class to generate an appointment for an interview.

Span of control. The number of subordinates a supervisor can handle effectively. Varies widely depending upon the capability of the supervisor, type of subordinates, complexity of the jobs, physical proximity, and amount of empire building permitted.

Voluntary termination. One of two ways employment is severed. Generally refers to leaving for a better position.

B. Develop your "action vocabulary."

The following seventy-two words should become part of your speech during the interview. They are the words of the winners in life, so belong to you.

While you can just photocopy the list and glance at it regularly, the best way to weave these words into your vocabulary is to write ten of them on your old business cards (or cut up some index cards) and place the cards in your wallet or purse. Take them out frequently during the first week and make up positive sentences about yourself, using one word per sentence. The following weekend, do the same with another ten words. Repeat this process until you have completed the entire list. You'll be amazed at the improvement in your speech and your attitude. Most important, you'll probably be hired long before this exercise is through.

Of course, there are other words, but these are the ones that get you hired:

Ability	Common sense	Dynamic
Accelerate	Conceive	Effective
Accurate	Conduct	Efficiency
Active	Conscientious	Eliminate
Affect	Control	Energetic
Aggressive	Develop	Enthusiastic
Analyze	Diplomatic	Establish
Attitude	Direct	Evaluate
Capable	Discipline	Excel
Careful	Drive	Excellence

Expand	Participate	Simplify
Expedite	Perform	Skill
Focus	Persuade	Solve
Generate	Potential	Streamline
Guide	Precise	Strengthen
Implement	Pride	Success
Improve	Produce	Systematic
Incisive	Professional	Tactful
Initiate	Proficiency	Thorough
Innovate	Provide	Train
Lead	Recommend	Trim
Listen	Reliable	Urgency
Monitor	Responsible	Vital
Motivate	Results	Win

Using these words is a great way to wake up a tired résumé and follow-up letter as well.

C. Internalize a few success phrases.

In his book *The Psychology of Winning,* Denis Waitley states:

> Perhaps the most important key to the permanent enhancement of self-esteem is the practice of positive self-talk. Every waking moment we must feed our subconscious self-images, positive thoughts about ourselves and our performances . . . so relentlessly and vividly that our self-images are in time modified to conform to the new, higher standards.
>
> Current research on the effect of words and images on the functions of the body offers amazing evidence of the power that words, spoken at random, can have on body functions monitored on bio-feedback equipment . . . that's why Winners rarely "put themselves down" in actions or words.[7]

You've just learned the winner's *vocabulary.* Success phrases are the winner's *motivation.* Here are some of my favorites:
You never fail, you just give up.
Work is not only the way to make a living, it's the way to make a life.

The people who succeed are the people who look for the opportunities they want; and if they don't find them, they make them.
We must be self-made, or never made.
We become not only what we think, but what we do.
As long as you stand in your own way, everything seems to be in your way.
Procrastination is a roadblock in the path of success.
When you try hard, you are almost there.
We become not what we think, but what we do.
The hardest work in life is resisting laziness.
A glimpse of an opportunity is an opportunity wasted.
The best investment you can make is in yourself.

Initially, the suggestion of internalizing success phrases may appear unimportant. Perhaps you'll discover other quotes (try *Bartlett's Familiar Quotations*) that mean even more to you. Or maybe you'll want to invent some yourself. But use them and you'll feel your self-confidence bloom. Include them in self-hypnosis tapes. Tell some to yourself in the mirror at home. Rehearse a few in your mind while you're having coffee before your interview. Find the right time during the interview to slip one in, and the interviewer will sit up and take notice. Success is catching!

D. Attempt to sit next to the interviewer.

You still might end up across the desk, but at least try, even if you have to come around it to "look at this together." This positioning invokes a classic management principle: "*You* and *me* against the problem," instead of "*you* against *me*." If a couch is in the office, stand there until you are asked to be seated, since that would be the best place for your interview. Occasionally you get the chance to have the interviewer sit on your favored side (i.e., your right side if you are right-handed). Grab it (not him). Your power position is greatly enhanced.

E. Subtly pick up the interviewer's body language, facial expressions, eye movement, rate of speech, tone of voice, and rate of breathing.

You use this technique all the time with people you meet. However, the results of conscious practice will amaze and amuse you. Subtle imitating, or "mirroring," is a way to establish rapport. But beware of the impulse to do literal imitation or you might both be walking out the door. This technique is designed only to *align, not to offend.* As you become accustomed to it, imitation becomes synonymous with agreement.

F. Present your résumé only if asked.

You want to appear organized, but it has already served its purpose.

G. Find an area of agreement, and start to lead very slowly toward the offer.

Leaning forward slightly in your seat at this phase is very effective. Typical statements you should use are:
 "My background fits this position well."
 "We have a good match here."
 "This looks like a long-term situation."
 "I'm excited about the position."
 "Everything looks good."

These statements close in on the interviewer without him realizing it. The next move is his.
 You're starting to turn the tide.

8. SAY POSITIVE THINGS ABOUT YOUR PRESENT (OR LAST) EMPLOYER.

I know it won't be easy. It never is! Let's face it, human beings were simply not made to work for each other. There is an enormous amount of latent hostility in the employment relationship, even under the best of circumstances. Anyone who has conducted exit interviews can attest to that.
 Almost every motivational and self-help authority has recognized that there is a difference between the words used by winners and losers. That's why buzzwords, action vocabulary, and

success phrases get you hired. So be positive in your statements.

Another reason to rehearse a positive statement is that the interviewer may interpret negative comments as revealing inappropriate information about your present (or last) employer. You risk the possibility that he will anticipate the same treatment if you are hired.

Your leather lunch box isn't the only baggage you're bringing into the interview. Your image is closely connected with your background. Even if your former employer was a loser, accentuate the positive.

I had a colleague who was treated very badly by his former employer and was justifiably angry. But he let this anger show when he went for a job interview. When he didn't get the job, he was sure his ex-employer had blackballed him. He was wrong. He shot himself in the foot by speaking negatively about his old boss—and therefore himself.

There is always a tendency to justify your reason for being in the office by blaming your present (or last) employer, but remember Dr. Waitley's advice:

Winners focus on past successes and forget past failures. They use errors and mistakes as a way to learning—they dismiss them from their minds.

. . . Winners know it doesn't matter how many times they have failed in the past. What matters is their successes which should be remembered, reinforced, and dwelt upon.[8]

9. ADMIRE THE ACHIEVEMENTS OF THE EMPLOYER.

Surely I don't need to convince you that flattery will get you everywhere. People appreciate honest and sincere praise (even if you don't mean it).

Use the information you acquired through your research and listening to mention the successes of the employer, as evidenced by the number of employees, business locations, products, sales, profits, future plans, and a variety of other elements.

Mention that the anticipated expansion of the organization will create new opportunities. State that multiple locations mean a chance to combine resources and bring continuity to overall operations. Its products must be liked by others, or they wouldn't be in business; find out why and note it. Sales and profits are impressive if they're up. If they're down, it's because they need more superstars like you. Future plans are exciting challenges, and you're ready for them.

These are the ways to tie the employer to you. No "canned" sales pitch is necessary. Just look for opportunities to sell yourself.

10. BE EXTREMELY OBSERVANT.

At this point, approximately 80 percent of the interview is over. Most of your anxiety is gone, and you may be getting bored. Your central nervous system will be stabilizing and may reduce your metabolic rate below normal. But the halo effect must be maintained. After all, we want more than just an acquaintance . . . we want a *friend*!

You should be using your antennae at this stage: you are looking and listening . . . receiving data for processing in the followup letter. Names, titles, buzzwords, products, and other input.

A successful interview requires extraordinary attentiveness, and that earlier cup of coffee or tea should be working for you right about now.

Sometimes people have the urge to assess the interviewer's state of mind during the interview. My technique, developed in litigation, is the "smile count." I mentally note the number of times a judge smiles at me and subtract the number of times opposing counsel obtains this acknowledgment. It works. In addition, I have perfected my smile and a number of jokes while keeping score. Proper use of good-natured humor breaks down the barriers so you can move in.

11. PROJECT AN IMAGE WITH STAYING POWER.

We are now in the final stages of the interview and you will soon be gone. Studies consistently show that within an hour after your departure, up to *85 percent* of your words will be forgotten. The only tangible things left from your encounter will be the documents you submitted and perhaps a few notes.

Therefore, the best way to approach this final phase of the interview is to determine what to pack into that 15 percent. You want to be identified as possessing four major attributes:

Enthusiasm
Confidence
Energy
Dependability

If you're penetrating with direct hits regarding these personality traits, you'll be far ahead of the applicant who just arrived for the next interview.

In addition, there are four subsidiary attributes that should be stressed when interviewing for any position:

Loyalty
Honesty
Pride in work
Service for value received

In professional, management, administrative, and clerical positions, you can add the last four:

Efficiency
Procedures
Economy
Profit

12. THE MAGIC FOUR GOOD-BYE.

The Magic Four Good-bye is exactly the same as the Magic Four Hello, with the exception of the third item.

1. A smile.
2. Direct eye contact.
3. The words, "It sounds like a great opportunity . . . I look forward to hearing from you."
4. A firm but gentle handshake.

In practicing the irresistible interview technique, there are ten things that you absolutely should not do. They are:

1. DON'T WAIT OVER THIRTY MINUTES FOR THE IN-TERVIEWER.

This is too long and anxiety becomes anger. You'll also be coming down from the psychomotor peak from the anticipation of a half hour earlier. Politely tell the receptionist you can't wait more than fifteen minutes longer. Make sure she notifies the interviewer immediately.

If you go through with the interview, do it for practice only, because that is all you will get.

2. DON'T WEAR A COAT, HAT, OR OTHER OUTDOOR CLOTHING.

Remove any outer garments in the reception area. Wearing them psychologically separates you from the interviewer, makes you appear to be a stranger, and gives the impression that either you were late or want to leave. All of these vibes are negative. If possible, also avoid taking them with you into the inner office. Doing so is awkward and distracting.

3. DON'T WEAR SUNGLASSES.

You will be eliminating one of your most important devices: direct eye contact. This and your impersonal look will ensure that you won't be hired.

4. DON'T ADDRESS THE INTERVIEWER BY HIS FIRST NAME.

It should always be either "Mr." or "Ms." unless you are asked to be more familiar. If he calls you by your first name, ask whether he minds if you reciprocate.

5. DON'T SMOKE OR CHEW GUM.

Asking for permission is the same as apologizing. Even if the interviewer consents, smoke is the last thing you want in the office. In many offices today, smoking is prohibited. Even if it is not, smokers don't realize the offensive odor tobacco leaves on their breath, hair, hands, and clothes. They also have higher health risks, raising sick leave, disability, and group medical insurance payments dramatically. Therefore, even if the interviewer smokes, you shouldn't.

Since this is no time to quit, buy nonsmoking tablets or patches. Read the label, and choose a product that has no warnings about blood pressure, heart conditions, or drowsiness. Those that do, generally contain either stimulants or sedatives that can affect your reactions. Try out the tablets or patches a few days before the interview so you will be able to judge if there is any difference in how you feel.

As for chewing gum, don't. It just looks tacky.

6. DON'T INTERRUPT THE INTERVIEWER.

Jobseekers often move fast and talk fast. They interrupt interviewers while they're talking, either to move them along or to impress them with their knowledge. If you find yourself interrupting the interviewer, recognize that you are out of sync and bring yourself back to the pacing level.

7. DON'T OBJECT TO DISCRIMINATORY QUESTIONS.

Answer them as good-naturedly as you can. Don't even mention that you know they're illegal. This is no time to display your knowledge or your anger.

8. DON'T LOOK AT YOUR WATCH DURING THE INTERVIEW.

This indicates that you are anxious, puts pressure on the interviewer, and interferes with the rapport that should be developing.

9. DON'T READ ANY DOCUMENTS ON THE INTERVIEWER'S DESK.

This is not only bad manners, it is meddling in something that is not your concern. Even if the information is interesting, avoid the temptation. The only exception is publications or other documents obviously intended to impress candidates. Admire them.

10. DON'T PICK UP ANY OBJECTS IN THE INTERVIEWER'S OFFICE.

Many people closely identify with the objects in their office. They often feel they are extensions of themselves. Even if nothing is said, this is never appreciated, and causes some interviewers to terminate the interview early, without comment. And you know what *that* means!

CHAPTER V

The Interrogation Interview: Hope It Happens

Technological advances and economic chaos have occupationally displaced record numbers of Americans. This has resulted in a virtually permanent "buyer's market," with the prospect of full employment nothing more than a dream of the past. In this environment, the "interrogation interview" is common. Interrogation interviews always contain a number of offensive questions designed to place you on the defensive.

Sometimes, this is an attempt to test your ability to react to stress. (In fact interrogation interviews are also known as "stress interviews.") Other times, it reflects the interviewer's response to stress.

At its worst, the interrogation interview may have a physical setting right out of a police scenario: a smoke-filled room, inadequate lighting, improper air conditioning, uncomfortable temperature, and, of course, a hard-back chair that squeaks. More subtle interviewers create the same effect simply by sitting in front of a bright window so that the glare puts you at a disadvantage.

That's the "Interrogation Interview" half of the title. The "Hope It Happens" part arises because you will *absolutely shine*! You will be so far ahead of the competition that your bloodshot eyes will be filled with tears of joy as you arrange for the preemployment physical.

Scores of people through the years have taken my advice and have virtually brought interrogation interviewers to their knees. The trick is so simple, it's amazing that other people don't use it. I can picture an interviewer with his chin stretched over his desk, begging some candidate to accept the offer he's extending for the position.

Gaining confidence in this situation is just a matter of practicing answering difficult questions in front of a mirror, with a tape recorder running. The typical interrogatories below are some of the questions you may be asked. The answers demonstrate the technique, but must be honest for you. If you decide to rehearse your own answers, be sure that you come out of each one neutralizing the sting of the question. Of course, adapt the actual wording to your own way of speaking.

Remember, you want to sound as though you were thinking of the question yourself. Answer in a sincere, direct manner, and move through the volley as quickly as courtesy will allow, so you can transform the interrogation interview into the irresistible interview.

The questions and answers are as follows:

1. WHY ARE YOU LEAVING YOUR PRESENT POSITION?

A. I'm interested in additional responsibility and learning more about the area of _____. The opportunity in my present position is limited because of the: (a) size of the company, (b) limited product line, (c) emphasis of the company on other areas.

2. HOW FAR DO YOU THINK YOU CAN GO IN COMPANY X? WHY?

A. Eventually, I'd like to work my way up to being _____. Of course, this will depend upon a number of factors. I think the environment in Company X is conducive to developing its employees. Your _____, _____, and _____ are all excellent. I'm interested in contributing to its goals and know my efforts will be recognized.

3. WHAT ARE YOU LOOKING FOR IN A JOB?

A. I've found that as with everything else, you get out of something what you put into it. I also know that every job has its challenges. Therefore, the position of _____ should provide the opportunity I'm seeking.

4. WHAT ARE YOUR CAREER OBJECTIVES?

A. I'm looking for a company where I can contribute to its goals. Company X has a reputation for rewards commensurate with your performance. Therefore, my career objectives are to work my way into a _____ position. I want to learn as much as I can, so that as opportunities for advancement arise, I'll be ready.

5. WHY SHOULD WE HIRE YOU?

A. I've talked with several of your employees and know Company X by reputation. It appears to be a good match and would probably result in a long-term relationship.

6. WHAT CAN YOU DO FOR US THAT SOMEONE ELSE CANNOT DO?

A. My references are the best people for you to ask. But I think they would agree that I believe in doing my best at whatever I do. Not everyone I've worked with does this.

7. DO YOU LIKE TO WORK? WHY?

A. Yes. There is a saying, "Work is not only the way to make a living, it's the way to make a life." It's true. My livelihood is an important part of my life. I'm a work-oriented person, and really enjoy being a _____.

8. WHAT KIND OF SALARY ARE YOU WORTH?

A. This should be relative to my contribution to Company X. While I expect an increase to make a move, I'm sure you'll be fair.

9. WHAT WERE YOUR FIVE BIGGEST ACCOMPLISHMENTS IN YOUR LAST JOB?

A._____

_____

_____

10. WHAT WERE YOUR FIVE BIGGEST ACCOMPLISH-MENTS IN YOUR CAREER?

A._____

_____

_____

11. CAN YOU WORK UNDER PRESSURE, DEADLINES, ETC.?

A. I've been particularly successful at working under pressure. For example, in my last position _____. You're in a competitive business, and deadlines are a way of life.

12. WHAT KINDS OF PEOPLE DO YOU LIKE?

A. I like people I can trust. My friends are from all walks of life, but they have two things in common: dependability and personal integrity. I'm very fortunate.

13. WHAT KINDS OF PEOPLE DO YOU DISLIKE?

A. People who say one thing and do another. Differences of opinion will occur, but honestly discussing them with the other person can go a long way toward resolving them.

14. WHY DIDN'T YOU DO BETTER IN SCHOOL?

A. I was involved with other activities and growing up. I always got along with my teachers and classmates. I even won a _____, _____, and was recognized by _____.

15. WHY DID YOU CHANGE JOBS SO FREQUENTLY?

A. I really didn't plan it that way. At _____, it was a matter of simply no opportunity to advance. My manager was an excellent teacher, and delegated duties to me regularly. I simply outgrew the position. When I was at _____, the company was purchased by

_____, and the office was closed. I then went to _____, and planned to grow with the company. However, when _____ learned about my experience, they recruited me away with a 20 percent increase and exciting long-range plans for the company and myself. Unfortunately, the market for _____ has changed and my career could not develop further there.

16. WHAT IS YOUR BIGGEST STRENGTH?

A. I think my ability to get the job done is my biggest strength. I take great pride in accomplishing something efficiently, on time, and with no errors. I'm also a "team player" and relate to people at different levels.

17. WHAT IS YOUR BIGGEST WEAKNESS?

A. Sometimes my _____ tells me I'm *too* concerned about doing a good job. I suppose that could be viewed as a strength though.

18. WHAT MAKES YOU ANGRY?

A. I don't get angry at other people very often, and am considered very patient by those who know me. If I had to find something, it would probably be working with someone who intentionally does not do his job properly. If you're getting paid you owe it to your employer, the customer, and yourself to do your best.

19. HOW LONG WOULD IT TAKE YOU TO MAKE A CONTRIBUTION TO OUR COMPANY?

A. Probably right away. I know what I'm doing, learn quickly, and expect a lot from myself.

20. HOW LONG WOULD YOU STAY WITH OUR COMPANY?

A. From all I've been able to determine, this should be for a long time. The personality of Company X appears to match my own, and I think the relationship would work out well.

21. ARE YOU WILLING TO TRAVEL?

A. Yes. I have a great family that understands "business is business." I'm used to traveling and have learned to adapt to living out of a suitcase.

22. ARE YOU WILLING TO RELOCATE?

If you are: Yes. I can't think of any region in the country that I would not accept. After all, every inner city has its suburbs. The only real differences are the weather and the accents. My family can always return to _____ to visit.

If you are not: Not unless the opportunity is really exceptional, since it would mean uprooting my family. However, I'd like to keep my options open. If the potential is there, I'll consider it seriously.

23. WHAT POSITION DO YOU EXPECT TO HAVE IN FIVE YEARS?

A. This depends not only upon my work performance, but also on the growth of Company X. However, I hope to be in a position of responsibility in the _____ area.

24. WHAT DO YOU THINK OF YOUR PREVIOUS BOSS?

A. I like my manager, and appreciate the opportunity he gave me to be productive. My reasons for leaving relate more to the circumstances of not being able to use my potential.

25. WHY HAVEN'T YOU OBTAINED A JOB SO FAR?

A. I've received a number of offers. However, an opportunity like this has not been available.

26. WHAT ACTIVITIES IN YOUR PREVIOUS JOBS HAVE YOU LIKED?

A._____
_____
_____

27. WHAT ACTIVITIES IN YOUR PREVIOUS JOBS HAVE YOU DISLIKED?

A._____
_____
_____

28. WOULD YOU DESCRIBE A FEW SITUATIONS IN WHICH YOUR WORK WAS CRITICIZED?

A. I don't remember any major criticism. If anything, I've been complimented on my work regularly. . . . Oh, yes, once someone made a comment about _____, but _____.

29. HOW DO YOU REACT TO CRITICISM?

A. I like to think about suggestions for improvement so I can respond intelligently rather than just reacting instinctively. Then, I arrange to discuss any criticism, determine the extent to which it is valid, and then identify specific steps I can take to improve my performance.

30. WHAT WAS THE LAST BOOK YOU READ?

A. (If you're not a nonfiction reader, read a popular how-to book to discuss—no, not *this* one!)

31. WHAT WAS THE LAST MOVIE YOU SAW?

A. (If you're not a regular moviegoer, mention a popular G-rated film that was recently shown on television.)

32. WHAT INTERESTS YOU MOST ABOUT THIS POSITION?

A. The opportunity it presents for someone to _____.

33. WHAT INTERESTS YOU LEAST ABOUT THIS POSITION?

A. I don't really see anything that wouldn't be interesting.

34. DON'T YOU FEEL YOU MIGHT BE BETTER OFF IN A DIFFERENT TYPE OF COMPANY?

A. Not that I can see. I've evaluated Company X fully. The overall environment and the position you are offering make it particularly attractive.

35. WHY AREN'T YOU EARNING MORE MONEY?

A. I suppose everybody wants to earn more money. However, job satisfaction and long-range opportunity are important, too.

36. WILL YOU BE OUT TO TAKE YOUR BOSS'S JOB?

A. No. However, part of my job is to help my supervisor advance with Company X. I should also be learning so I can eventually do that job. To that extent, I might be after his job—but he might be after the one above his!

37. ARE YOU CREATIVE? GIVE AN EXAMPLE.

A. Yes. Every job can be done better. For example, in my last position, I _____.

38. ARE YOU ANALYTICAL? GIVE AN EXAMPLE.

A. Yes. Analytical capability is an important part of being a good _____. For example, in my last position, I _____.

39. HOW WOULD YOU DESCRIBE YOUR PERSONALITY?

A. Even-tempered. There are two sides to every question, and I've found that a lot more can be accomplished by people working together. I always try to look at things as "*you* and *me* against the problem," rather than "*you* against *me.*"

40. WHAT DO YOU LIKE TO DO IN YOUR SPARE TIME?

A. I read a lot in the _____ field. It helps me to be more effective _____, and I can bring new ideas to the job. I also spend time doing _____, since I enjoy my work even when I'm not getting paid. Of course, I really enjoy my family as well.

41. HOW IS YOUR FAMILY LIFE?

A. Excellent. My family is very supportive. This makes it all worthwhile.

42. WHAT DO YOUR SUBORDINATES THINK OF YOU?

A. They respect me and understand we have a job to do. I try to recognize them for their achievements and have trained them to take over when I'm not there. They appreciate that.

43. CAN YOU DELEGATE RESPONSIBILITY? GIVE AN EXAMPLE.

A. Yes. This is an important part of being a manager. First it's necessary to train your subordinates so they can assume the responsibility delegated. For example, in my last position I _____.

44. HAVE YOU HIRED PEOPLE BEFORE? WHAT DO YOU LOOK FOR?

If you did: Yes. I look for a dedication to work and a willingness to learn. The ability to get along with others is also important, because "no man is an island."

If you did not: Not directly. However, I was asked my opinion about candidates. I'd look for a dedication to work and a willingness to learn. The ability to get along with others is also important, because "no man is an island."

45. HAVE YOU FIRED PEOPLE BEFORE? WHAT REASONS CAUSED YOU TO DO SO?

If you did: Yes. Generally for poor work performance. I tend to expect a lot, and let's face it, not everyone is dedicated to quality.

If you did not: Not directly. However, I was often asked my opinion on other employees' work performance. It's not easy to say something negative about a coworker, but the supervisors knew I expected a lot. Let's face it, a dedication to quality is best for everyone.

46. WHAT ARE THE TYPES OF JOBS YOU ARE CONSIDERING?

A. (Review the activities of the job Company X is offering.)

47. WHAT OTHER COMPANIES ARE YOU CONSIDERING?

A. I'd rather not say, because they have expressed an interest in hiring me. They are companies a lot like Company X, however.

48. WHAT SIZE COMPANY DO YOU PREFER TO WORK FOR?

A. It really makes no difference. However, the size of Company X seems to combine the best of both worlds, because _____.

49. TELL US ALL ABOUT YOURSELF. HOW IS YOUR HEALTH?

A. I was raised in _____, and graduated from _____ in _____. I was recruited by _____, and have held progressively more responsible positions in the _____ field. My health is excellent.

50. MAY WE CONTACT YOUR PRESENT EMPLOYER?

A. Yes, after we've agreed on the job I'll be doing. For obvious reasons, I'd appreciate that contact not be made until then. It's likely I'll receive a counteroffer and would prefer to be the first to tell them. They would appreciate that, I'm sure.

51. MAY WE CONTACT YOUR REFERENCES?

A. Yes, once mutual interest has been established. I've selected successful people who know my personal and professional qualifications well, but I don't want to impose on them. Just let me know when you need the contact information, and I'll provide it.

52. DO YOU SPEAK A FOREIGN LANGUAGE?

If you do: Yes.
  If you do not: I studied _____ in high school/college and enjoyed it.

53. DO YOU PREFER WORKING WITH A TEAM OR WOULD YOU RATHER WORK ALONE?

A. You have to be able to work well as a team member, but it's just as important to be able to work independently when necessary. I can do both equally well.

54. WHAT DO YOU THINK IS MOST IMPORTANT TO SUCCESS?

A. You have to give 100 percent in your efforts. Personal satisfaction and the ability to meet and exceed your own internal goals and expectations have to be as important to you as impressing management.

55. DO YOU LIKE TO WORK WITH PEOPLE?

A. Yes, because there is a synergy in teamwork that is exciting. I like to see people working together toward a common objective. The energy and creativity they generate as a team far exceeds what they could have accomplished as individuals.

56. ARE YOU AFRAID TO FLY?

A. Not at all. The speed of air travel is necessary to expedite business, and I've traveled on a regular basis in my previous positions.

57. WOULD YOU BE WILLING TO TAKE A LIE DETECTOR TEST AND/OR A DRUG TEST?

A. Yes. I have nothing to hide, although I'd like to know the purpose of the test if it is a requirement of employment here, and I'd like to be assured of its accuracy.

58. HOW WELL DO YOU COPE WITH STRESS?

A. Stress is an inevitable part of living, but I cope with it well. I eat properly, exercise, and try to get enough rest. When I feel pressured at work, I also find it helpful to think back on my many successes and the obstacles I've overcome in the past. These memories calm me and make me feel confident.

59. IF YOU DISAGREED WITH YOUR MANAGER, WOULD YOU SPEAK UP?

A. I'm not a "yes man," but I'm careful when I disagree with my manager. I think my position through thoroughly, use speech that is constructive rather than confrontational, and present my position privately.

60. ARE YOU INNOVATIVE?

A. Yes. I have common sense that I've applied during my career to make things work more efficiently and effectively. I also have the ability to draw out the talents of other people and tap into their creativity as well.

61. DO YOU HAVE ANY BIASES OR PREJUDICES?

A. I'm biased against people who don't work hard and try to do their best. I give 100 percent of my effort, and I expect my colleagues to do the same.

62. ARE YOU AGGRESSIVE?

A. I'm assertive rather than aggressive. I don't push people around to get my way. I prefer a two-way exchange where no one is attacked. I like to make my ideas known forcefully but without demeaning others.

63. ARE YOU A SELF-STARTER?

A. Yes. I always set expectations for myself that go beyond those set by my managers. If I know what needs to be done, I don't need a request from someone else to do it. It's still my responsibility.

64. WHAT DO YOU THINK IT TAKES TO BE SUCCESS-FUL?

A. The most important thing is the motivation to do things better today than you did yesterday and to become even better tomorrow. You have to expect a lot of yourself and constantly strive to improve upon your past accomplishments.

65. HOW DO YOU MAKE IMPORTANT DECISIONS?

A. I gather all of the information I need, including input from others. I then make a list of all available alternatives, with the advantages, disadvantages, and requirements of each. I rely on my past experience and intuition before making a choice.

66. HOW WOULD YOU ESTABLISH RAPPORT WITH YOUR STAFF?

A. I would first have to know all I can about each staff member, personally and professionally, so I would do a lot of listening . . . meeting with them on a one-to-one basis for the dialogue so critical to a successful working relationship.

67. HOW IMPORTANT IS THE ABILITY TO DELEGATE?

A. The ability to delegate responsibility is critical to managerial success. You have to first select competent staff and then train them to do what is required. Once this is done, you have to let go and give them the opportunity to serve you well.

68. WHAT DO YOU THINK YOU'LL BE DOING FIVE YEARS FROM NOW?

A. I see myself working for this company. In five years, I should be able to look back over a number of contributions I've made and innovations I've introduced. I'll be higher in the organization than I am now and looking forward to making continued contributions.

69. WHEN WOULD YOU EXPECT A PROMOTION?

A. I expect to progress in my career, but I know that promotions have to be earned. First, I will have to master my new position, institute improvements, take on the added responsibilities, perform them well, and then train someone to take over my job. Then, and only then, will I expect a promotion. At that time, I will have earned it.

70. WHAT DO YOU KNOW ABOUT OUR COMPANY?

(Do your job research before the interview: see Chapter X. Single out three positive facts about the company, refer to recent company developments, and link your skills to their mission.)

71. WHY SHOULD WE GIVE YOU THIS JOB AND WHY DO YOU WANT IT?

A. I am exceptionally well qualified for this position. My skills, training, and experience are directly related to the position. I'm dedicated, highly motivated, and a quick learner. I've researched your company, and I like the way you've progressed and the way you see the future. I know I would fit in well.

72. CAN YOU GIVE ME FIVE REASONS FOR YOUR SUCCESS?

A. I am skilled, have a high level of energy, and am very productive. My work is consistently exceptional. I like challenges and continue to improve my skills and abilities. I am innovative and am good at looking at old problems and formulating creative solutions. I am highly responsible and take my job very seriously.

73. ARE YOU COMPUTER LITERATE?

A. Yes. While I'm not an expert, I've been exposed to various computer systems and applications through my work and have tracked the development of this technology on my own initiative.

74. DO YOU KNOW HOW TO NAVIGATE THE INTERNET?

A. Yes. I use it extensively for research and to watch my company's competitors. I check out their websites and various business-related sites to identify new developments and track their progress.

75. WHAT ARE THE SPECIAL CHALLENGES ASSOCIATED WITH FINDING AND KEEPING A JOB IN TODAY'S JOB MARKET?

A. Intense competition and downsizing have become an accepted part of our economy. In order to succeed in this job market, candidates must be increasingly vigilant to know about new developments, update their skills, and present their capabilities in new ways. This is especially true for older employees who must often change careers in midlife. The challenge is there, and it can be met.

These answers work consistently to turn interviews into jobs. You should ask the interviewer some questions as well. Here are some examples of questions to ask:

- What are your company's plans for expansion?
- Is the department a profit center?
- How important are the department's functions to senior management?
- Are you ready and able to hire now?
- How long has the position been open?
- How many employees have held the position in the last five years?
- Why are the former employees no longer in the position?
- How many employees have been promoted from the position in the past five years?
- What does management consider to be the five most important duties of the position?
- What do you expect the person you hire to accomplish?

Like I say . . . hope your interview happens.

CHAPTER VI

The Second Time Around: Once More with Feeling

The second interview is often equated with getting the job. Statistically, this is true about 60 percent of the time. However, there are crucial differences from your first visit. If you understand them, you can increase your chances of being hired to almost a certainty.

If your first interview was with the human resources department, you will often be asked to return for another meeting. This will probably be with the supervisor and others in the department that has the job opening, i.e., with the functional department.

Let me guide you through this obstacle course. If you have already made direct contact with the supervisor, and your second interview is with the human resources department, then you've probably already won the battle. That second interview is merely a formality. Watching someone use a rubber stamp doesn't require much training.

As used in this chapter, *supervisor* means any functional hiring authority from the chief executive officer on down.

The differences are subtle. Perhaps that is why my prolific colleagues don't discuss them. Generally, you have passed through the interviewer's office and will be working on your future supervisor. This means that you *must* use every means at your disposal to understand what makes him tick.

At this point, you should have several acquaintances within the company whom you can contact. If you haven't developed them, now is the time.

One ally you probably have overlooked is the interviewer himself. He has stamped you with his seal of approval, and you can help him by closing the requisition. The interviewer also knows that if he allows too many applicants to become actual candidates, the supervisor will delay making a decision. With so many seemingly qualified people, the supervisor's decision is that much more difficult.

Call the interviewer, and after expressing your appreciation, lead into the discussion with a comment something like: "From what I understand, it looks like I'll really be able to assist _____. Is there anything I should know before we meet?"

Then listen and take notes. The interviewer will be delighted to give you his impressions. Often they are extremely incisive, since he has access to the personnel files. Before you conclude the conversation, ask the interviewer if he thinks the supervisor would mind a direct call. Interpret his "No, I don't" as a suggestion that you do so.

Then call the supervisor. After saying that the interviewer suggested you call him and asking if he has a few minutes, state: "I'm looking forward to meeting you (again) on _____, at _____. Before we get together, I wonder if there's anything you'd like me to bring."

The supervisor will not be able to think that fast. In the remote event he asks for something, evaluate whether it can affect your chances adversely. If so, say something like: "I'll check to see if I have it. If not, I'll bring what I can."

This is more than just an excuse to confirm the interview. It is a chance to hear where the supervisor's thinking is going with regard to hiring you. A little industrial espionage goes a long way. And you don't have far to go.

Generally, the second interview is more *directed*. It takes one of two paths.

1. WHO ARE YOU?

Here we are, back at another irresistible interrogation interview. Except that now, you have already developed a profile of your target (with a little help from your friends). Just keep your powder dry and follow the same approach contained in Chapters IV and V. You'll blast right through.

After all, the supervisor is going to have a lot of explaining to do if you are rejected based upon subjective factors. If the interviewer hired the supervisor originally, bonding occurred and he will be in an even more powerful position to influence the outcome.

If you do not receive an offer, the *interviewer* will suffer a rejection shock seizure! It tends to abruptly straighten the backbone.

2. WHAT CAN YOU DO FOR US?

Time to dust off the old buzzwords given in Chapter IV, but really concentrate on the state-of-the-art words appropriate to the job you are considering. Hit the library and the Internet. Start building up your technical vocabulary, but don't use any words or phrases that you don't fully understand. All you need is a few choice phrases. This research should not require more than a couple of hours.

We're faced with more objective criteria here, and you should be able to anticipate the questions. The interview will tend to be informational rather than personal.

Since you may be introduced personally by the interviewer, the second interview may include him. It is up to you to create a "family atmosphere." Watch where you sit. Try to sit next to one or both of your "cousins." The interview will tend to be more familiar and unstructured because of the introduction and the fact that you are back again.

Don't be too physical, but a slightly warmer handshake and a possible hand on the small of the back as you're walking through the hall, one time only, will work wonders. Powerful thing, touching. But *only* if used sparingly!

You just can't lose with the stuff you use!

CHAPTER VII
Salary Requirements? "More!"

Unless this is your first job, or you are in a collective bargaining unit, you have experienced the trauma of asking for a raise. Generally, you receive one of three reactions:

1. THE "THIS IS YOUR LIFE" ROUTINE

This orchestration is usually conducted by the more intimidating boss, who calls you into his office, has your personnel folder, and looks you straight in the eye. Then he starts reading from The Book, droning a recital of all your faults, problems, and mistakes.

You are Dorothy and he is the wizard. If he only had a heart. But he doesn't, or as he would put it, "I'd love to help you but I can't."

2. THE "YOU KNOW HOW IT IS" ROUTINE

You are still called into the boss's office, where you watch him shrug his shoulders, writhe in pain about "company policy," or roll out the heavy "we're operating at a loss" artillery. It's sincerity time, but somehow the eye contact is just not there. Neither is the raise.

3. THE "SILENT TREATMENT" ROUTINE

This is designed to punish you for not waiting until the next scheduled review. The favorite technique is to ignore you by holding closed-door meetings near your work area with everyone else. Constant impersonal telephone calls about the status of different assignments are particularly effective as well. Sooner or later, you learn the "open door" only swings out. This one is the cruelest of all. Hope you escape without contracting paranoia.

These and other routines leave scars in your subconscious about your value in dollars long after the bruises heal. The programming in your mind translates asking for a higher salary into an unmentionable. "You should be ashamed, you *ingrate!*" you say to yourself. Unfortunately, too many people carry this feeling into a new situation as well.

For most people, the real gains in earnings will occur when they change jobs. It is unfortunate, but "good ol' boys" just don't get 20 percent increases and more unless they either threaten to leave or actually do. Onward really is upward!

In order to maximize your effectiveness at negotiating with the interviewer, you should reflect upon the salary soap operas that have victimized you in the past. If necessary, write down their scripts and relive them just long enough to understand that they really had nothing to do with your performance at all . . . only the way it was *perceived.* How do I know? Here's the secret: *The better the job you did, the more you felt you were entitled to the raise, and the worse you felt when you didn't get it.*

Negotiating a salary takes a completely opposite approach from asking for a raise. This is because it is an arm's-length transaction, and you are just an unread book with a quality cover.

This was pointed out to me on the day I was admitted to practice law in California. When I shaved that morning, I noticed a familiar face in the mirror. My father, a practicing attorney for almost half a century, had come out from New York to pop a few buttons on his vest. After the swearing-in ceremony, I asked Dad, "How will anyone know I'm an attorney?" He said, "They'll know, son. You won't even have to think about it. They'll know by the way you dress, the way you speak, and the way you carry yourself."

He was right. The most powerful messages are the ones you never say.

You should not disclose *any* salary on your résumé. You should also avoid any discussion of it during the interview. Interrogation interviewers may try to corner you, but the best answer is always that your salary should be relative to your contribution to the employer.

If you follow this advice long enough, you may actually find interviewers who *forget* to confirm the salary before extending the offer! This is not unusual, because your salary is one of the last things an interviewer is concerned about. And interviewers and supervisors can almost always stretch if they really want you.

Another reason to defer salary discussions in larger companies is to get past the employment interviewer and to the person you will be working for. This is because the human resources "mangler" is usually responsible for employment *and* wage and "slavery" administration. He has a vested interest in his *own* empire, and a love of procedures.

If you are fortunate enough to know the salary because it is in the interviewer's spiel, *don't react.* If you know through a telephone inquiry, advertisement, internal referral, placement service, or other source, acknowledge this, but again, *don't react.* Until you hear an absolute number, you are considering the options. Of course, it would be "inappropriate" to discuss other offers—downright "unprofessional," in fact. *Now,* who holds the reins?

Negotiating a salary is much like negotiating a loan: the more you look as if you need it, the less likely you are to get it.

Let the two precepts of the art of negotiating work for you: *the one who does the most talking ends up giving away the store;* and *the less you sweat, the more you get.*

Contemplate . . . let the interviewer negotiate . . . against himself. The question of whether you should ever disclose your present salary is something that you will have to decide for yourself. Salary is easy to verify by requiring proof from you (check stubs, tax returns, etc.) or contacting your present (or last) employer. Curiously enough, the higher the position, the less likely it is that anyone will check.

If you are prepared, the answer to a question about your salary can be creative. State the amount you will receive after your next review and your chances of receiving an increase. Overtime possibilities should also not be overlooked, since the wages are significantly higher than those paid for straight time. What about probable bonuses? What about other benefits? Consider pay in lieu of vacation, if that is available, since your new employer probably will not be allowing a vacation for a year. I am *not* recommending falsifying any information. I *am* recommending being aware of the hidden amounts that really add up. Remember, these are worth nothing if you don't include them, and 120 percent or more if you do (the amount of the actual salary plus the percentage of the increase you receive).

If the interviewer starts talking about your future to sell you on a lower salary, you should understand the game that is being played. Veterans at changing jobs know that the only future even remotely predictable is written in an employment agreement.

One final comment: You have to have the right mind-set during salary negotiations. You have to be willing to walk away from the deal. This doesn't mean you're *going* to walk, but you have to feel as though you would in order to stand firm in your demands and not be swayed into accepting the first salary offered.

CHAPTER VIII
References into Testimonials: Lovers Never Say Good-bye

During the past decade, statutory and case law in the areas of equal employment, unemployment insurance, consumer disclosure, credit reporting, libel, slander, privacy, interference with contractual relations, and wrongful termination has increased geometrically. This has led most corporate attorneys to advise against furnishing any references on behalf of former employees. As a result, many applicants have no professional references. Those that do are left with cautious, impersonal, passive accounts. Your ability to develop a cadre of interested, articulate, active advocates will be like opening your engine full throttle.

PERSONAL REFERENCES

As you can see from the buzzword definition of a personal reference contained in Chapter IV, the use of these references is limited because of their level of sophistication and the motivation to fabricate. However, you should not foreclose this option.

Select mature office employees with surnames different from yours as references. You don't want them to think you gave your father as a reference! Obtain their consent, and explain *exactly* what you would like them to say. Give them that high-class résumé of yours, a photocopy of a recent application, a list of the image factors found in Chapter IV, and the personal reference questions below to review before and during the telephone call.

We've all bought clothes we didn't like because the salesperson said they looked good. Third-party reinforcement is a powerful force, and you can drive up the credibility of these well-intentioned people dramatically by doing your homework.

Ask them to accept the telephone call requesting a reference or return it immediately, and notify you of the details the moment they hang up. (Remember our analysis of the ability to recall conversations in Chapter IV.) You need the feedback and you need it *fast*. At the very least, you will have presented some good character witnesses to help your case.

Personal Reference Questions

How long have you known _____?
How do you know _____?
What is your opinion of _____?
Is he easy to get along with?
Is he usually on time?
Was he absent from work very often?
Did he bring work home very often?
Did he like his last job?
What are his primary attributes?
What are his primary liabilities?

PROFESSIONAL REFERENCES

Cultivating professional (work-related) references is far more time-consuming and often involves reliving your sordid past. The rewards are great. Deep-Breath Phone Call time, just as we discussed in Chapter II.

If you're like most applicants, you've burned a few bridges along the way. Passive-aggressive references can be even more destructive than those who make negative comments, since the interviewer doesn't have the opportunity to consider the source. Former supervisors are often called without your permission or even knowledge, and you may be walking around under a cloud and not know it.

You know if you and your former supervisor didn't exactly need to be chiseled apart. That negative excess baggage is carried around in your unconscious, requiring that you rehearse a positive statement for the interviewer as described in Chapter IV. Don't let it stay in your memory center . . . call and make your peace as soon as possible with every former supervisor you can find. Let them know you *really* need them!

Professional references should be called, courted, and remembered during the holiday season. They share an important part of your life and can be a great source of guidance and perspective. Although the years and distance have separated us, I am still only a telephone call away from my first supervisor, and all that followed; two became dear friends . . . life is too short.

Work-related references are generally more potent than academic ones, because business wants tangible services. A bright, positive coworker can also be used effectively and will tend to identify with your needs. As with personal references, you should obtain their consent and review their "testimony." Don't let them use the old "Don't worry, I'll just tell them a bunch of lies" routine to get you off the phone. This is a *business* matter, and you will reciprocate.

Your résumé and a photocopy of a recent application (personal data is optional) should be forwarded to your references. Furnishing the image factors is important, since your message should be repeated to the interviewer. The professional reference questions that follow will complete the preparation. The procedure regarding immediate response to the interviewer's telephone call and "instant replay" to you is the same.

Professional Reference Questions

How long have you known _____?
How do you know _____?
Did you hire _____?
When was he hired?
When did he leave?
Why did he leave?
What was his salary when he left?
What were his titles?
Did you work with him directly?
Was he usually on time?
Was he absent from work very often?
What were his duties?

Did his personal life ever interfere with his work?
Did he cooperate with coworkers?
Did he cooperate with supervisors?
Did he take work home very often?
What are his primary attributes?
What are his primary liabilities?
Is he eligible for rehire?
Can you confirm the information he has given?

Friends may come and go, but *enemies remain*. Don't let them remain enemies.

CHAPTER IX
The Better Letter: Follow-up into Follow-through

The follow-up letter is the last step in getting hired. However, it is the single most effective postinterview technique you can use.

Follow-up letters are more than mere thank-you notes. They're a critical part of your strategy. The novice applicant either doesn't send them out at all or mumbles an apology for doing so. You are not a novice, and should be just itching to develop your follow-up letter.

All those words you said during the interview have dwindled down to one or two remarks, and your image is fading fast. The danger is that you will be grouped with other applicants. Now is the time to rekindle some of those fond old memories and restate your image.

The letter should be on high-quality personal letterhead, typed on a computer, fully addressed with no abbreviations, and contain the middle initial and title of the interviewer. It should be sent immediately after the interview. It should be brief, enthusiastic, and to the point.

Reiterate your primary assets and accomplishments, and convincingly describe how you can benefit the employer. Properly spell the names of people you met and include buzzwords familiar to the interviewer. It should end a lot like the words of the Magic Four Good-bye, requesting a reply as soon as possible.

Here are a few middle-of-the-road approaches for you to adapt. You can make them more formal or more highly personalized, depending on your sense of the character and personality of the interviewer.

Some things always to be included:

1. ADDRESS LINE

The full company name, full address (no abbreviations), full name of the interviewer and his full title. These make you look thorough and professional.

2. SUBJECT LINE

"Re: Interview for the Position of (title) on (date) ."
    This zeros in on the contents and dresses up the letter.

3. GREETING

"Dear Mr./Ms. (last name) ,"
    "Miss" or "Mrs." should not be used unless you know the interviewer does so. First names are out of the question even if they were used during the interview.

4. OPENING

   a. "It was a pleasure meeting with you last (day) to discuss
      the opening in (department) with Company X."
   b. "I appreciated meeting with (name) and yourself in your
      office on (day) to discuss the (title) position with Com-
      pany X."
   c. "Thanks again for taking the time to see me regarding the
      opening in (department) ."

Again, comment on or add to something discussed during your interview in the body of the letter. Choose a topic that allows you to emphasize directly or implicitly your qualifications. This will keep your follow-up from being just another routine thank-you.

5. BODY

    a. "From our discussion, and the fine reputation of your organization, it appears that the _(title)_ position would enable me to fully utilize my background in _____."

    b. "I was particularly impressed with the professionalism evident throughout my visit. Company X appears to have the kind of environment I have been seeking."

    c. "The atmosphere at Company X seems to strongly favor individual involvement, and I would undoubtedly be able to contribute significantly to its goals."

6. CLOSING

    a. "While I have been considering other situations, I have deferred a decision until I hear from you. Therefore, your prompt reply would be greatly appreciated."

    b. "It's an exciting opportunity, and I look forward to hearing your decision very soon."

    c. "The _(title)_ position and Company X are exactly what I have been seeking, and I hope to hear from you within the next week."

7. SALUTATION

"Sincerely,"
    "Very truly yours,"
    "Best regards,"

If you do not receive a response within a week, reread Chapter II, and modify the Deep-Breath Phone Call accordingly. If you have been interviewed by the decision maker rather than a human resources officer, a slightly different phone technique is used.

First, enlist the executive's secretary or assistant as your ally, not your adversary. A courteous, firm tone of voice works wonders. Don't play guessing games to get around the front desk: an executive calling an executive *always* states his name. Only nobodies have no names. And don't ask nosy questions about the boss's schedule, hoping to catch him unguarded. A good secretary simply will not tell you. In any case, if you call very early (before 9:00 A.M.) or late (after 5:00 P.M.), you can often get your man directly.

If you speak to the secretary:

SECRETARY:	Good morning, Mr. (*last name*)'s office.
YOU:	This is (*first name*) (*last name*) calling. May I speak to him, please?'
SECRETARY:	I'm sorry, he's stepped away from his desk/on another line/in a meeting. May I take a message?
YOU:	Mr. (*last name*) and I met last week regarding the (*title*) position.
SECRETARY:	One minute, please.

The boss might very well have stepped away from his desk, be on another line, or be in a meeting. But more than likely the secretary is checking to see if he wants to take the call or not. If not:

YOU:	When would be a good time to call back? (or) I'll hold, please.

Since you have been direct and helpful, the secretary is very likely to return the courtesy. Also be polite and stubborn: you'll get the decision maker and a decision before long.

Sometimes people with a sales background are surprised that I do not recommend "asking for the sale." This is because it is too easy to sound as if you are pleading when your livelihood is on the line. Instead, the pressure point is an *answer,* because you have "waited as long as you can," have "some decisions to make," etc.

In advising you on the approach to take, I have invoked the "fiddle theory" developed by Robert Ringer in his best-selling book *Winning Through Intimidation:*

> The longer a person fiddles around with something, the greater the odds that the result will be negative. . . . In the case of Nero, Rome burned; in the case of a sale, the longer it takes to get to a point of closing, the greater the odds that it will never close.

As a general rule, you should assume that time is always

against you when you try to make a deal—any kind of deal. There's an old saying about "striking while the iron's hot," and my experience has taught me that it certainly is a profound statement in that circumstances always seem to have a way of changing.[9]

Concentrate on a well-drafted letter as I have suggested, keep the pressure on the employer, and don't let the ball drop on your interview scheduling.

CHAPTER X

Job Hunting in the Internet Age: Untangling the Web

The Internet has permanently changed the job search arena.

Using the Internet to find terrific job opportunities can help you to:
- Scope out thousands of job openings worldwide.
- Submit your résumé online and invite an immediate response.
- Get free advice on everything from résumé preparation to salary negotiation.
- Research companies and employment trends.
- Contact other jobseekers to share information.

You can do this whenever you choose, 24/7, in the privacy of your own home using your computer.

Think it's hard? It's easy, *when you do it our way.* You'll be off the street and into the seat in no time . . . and you'll have fun doing it!

Sounds too good to be true? It is! Don't expect to get a job by using the Internet alone. Less than 2 percent of all people who apply for jobs listed on the Internet actually receive an offer. Eighty percent of all jobs are still filled through personal contacts and networking. One-on-one techniques for career success will never be replaced. Still, using the Internet can be invaluable in your job search. Let's see how the Internet can help you land the job of your dreams.

GETTING STARTED ON THE INTERNET

Love-hate attitudes toward computers notwithstanding, *you need a computer.* Without one, you can't access the Internet and you can't send and receive e-mail.

If you don't have a computer, buy one. It's a buyer's market, and you can get a new one with all of the features you need for under $600. Various software packages, often including a virus-protection program, are usually included in the purchase price. Another $100 or so will pay for a monitor. An additional $400 buys you the entire Microsoft Office software package, which includes word processing, spreadsheet, presentation, and mass-mailing capabilities. If you buy just Microsoft Word, the price is much less. You'll also need a printer—around $100—and a backup program in case your computer crashes (another $50). All of these expenditures are tax deductible.

If you *really* can't afford a PC, you can use computers free at a public library.

Learning to use a computer isn't as hard as it looks. Help is everywhere. There are private tutors and thousands of books, manuals, and built-in tutorials. Classes at local community colleges and adult education centers are also available.

A word of caution: Concentrate on learning the basics and don't get bogged down in mastering the more advanced aspects of computer use. Unless you plan to make computers your profession, you won't need these skills, and trying to perfect them will waste your valuable job-seeking time.

Another word of caution: Patience is as important as competence in an instructor. Computer experts often lack the patience to methodically lead you through the necessary steps. Don't let them intimidate you! If one instructor is moving too fast or refuses to answer questions, get a *different* instructor. There are thousands of them out there looking for your business.

Finally, to log on to the Internet, you need a *service provider* to initiate and maintain your connection, such as AOL or Earthlink. You also need a *browser* to access various sites. Netscape Navigator and Microsoft Explorer have captured the browser market. Your service provider will make them available to you as

part of your contract or will provide their own browser. Costs for
Internet service vary, but they can be as low as ten dollars a
month.

Now you're ready to surf!

USING THE INTERNET TO FIND JOBS

Websites and *search engines* help you navigate through the maze
of data found on the Internet.

Websites are addresses maintained by companies, government
agencies, associations, universities, and individuals. Anyone who
wants to advertise can do so through a website. Many of these are
designed to sell you a product or service. Others provide only information. Once you have a website address, you can go directly
to that site by clicking on it without navigating through the entire
Internet. Websites also contain links to other websites with related
information, which can be accessed by clicking on them with
your mouse.

Search engines are designed to help you locate information on
the Internet. Some of the more popular search engines are Google,
AltaVista, Yahoo, and Lycos. Once you access the search engine's
website, you type in certain key words or phrases, click on the
"search" button, and get a list of citations pertaining to your key
words. Click on the highlighted text in these citations, and the information comes up on your screen. Most search engines also
have a Boolean feature, enabling you to enter certain phrases in
quotes and to specify which search words should be included.
This narrows your search and increases the possibility of finding
the exact information you need.

Once you've mastered these features, the Internet can help you
in your job search by:
- Letting you conduct research on companies, industries,
  and the labor market.
- Making you aware of thousands of job openings and opportunities.
- Giving you the capability of responding to these opportunities immediately.
- Receiving an immediate response in turn.

RESEARCHING COMPANIES AND THE JOB MARKET

Never go to a job interview without doing research on the company. You should know something about its history, its services, and its competitors. You should know the state of the industry, recent trends in the field, and recent developments in the company.

This is important because *you have to stand out from the crowd.*

Put yourself in the employer's position. Which candidate would impress you more? The candidate whose responses are limited to a routine recitation of what he's done in the past, or the candidate who already *knows* what your company does, the names of your competitors, and how you have fared in the market? Discuss three trends in the industry that you think are important. Mention something you've read about the firm in a recent news story. Have there been any innovative breakthroughs in the field? Weave them into your conversation. Want to impress the interviewer even more? Using this background information, tell him how your capabilities would benefit the company.

The main thing a prospective employer is looking for when he interviews an applicant is a positive answer to the question, "What can you do for me?" Doing your homework about the company puts you in a position to answer this question with conviction. Taking the time to do this research shows the employer that you have thought about why you want the job and how you might fit into his company. You haven't answered the ad just because you need a paycheck. He sees that you're excited about the opportunity and willing to go the extra mile. You stand out from the competition.

Finding this information used to be difficult. You'd spend hours in the library battling with card catalogs, reference books, and microfiche machines. You'd wander through archive files and book stacks. You might find the names of people who could tell you something about the company, then you'd try to get that information from reluctant administrative assistants.

All of this has changed. Thanks to the Internet, finding this information has never been easier. Just log on and the business world is at your fingertips. (See pages 17 and 84–86 for lists of useful research sites.)

The Internet has many resources with information about companies you might wish to consider. These sites provide valuable information including the company's mission, products, and services offered, key officials, recent press releases, etc. Read their mission statement. Look at their strategic plan and annual report. See the "What's New" section of their website for information on recent developments. Then use this information to point out how your special skills can help them to move in a positive direction. You can supplement this information by using search engines to access financial publications, business magazines, and newspapers for articles and stories about the target company.

Useful job data available on the Internet goes far beyond information on specific companies. It can also provide you with an in-depth knowledge of industry trends. You can find out which industries, and what jobs within them, are growing the fastest. You can research salary developments by industry, occupation, or position.

Information is also available on cost-of-living differences in various regions to help you decide if you want to relocate and seek employment in another city. Databases such as On-Net and the websites of the Bureau of Labor Statistics and the Census Bureau provide comprehensive information on national, state, and local population trends; job markets; average income by occupation; housing costs; relocation considerations; and other vital data so critical to a serious job search.

FINDING OPPORTUNITIES

The Internet gives you full access to literally thousands of jobs through *job banks* or *résumé banks*. One of the largest of these is monster.com, but there are hundreds of them out there.

Job or résumé banks are websites designed to bring candidates and jobs together. They often contain tens of thousands of résumés and job openings in their database. Jobseekers post their résumés on this site and respond to job listings free of charge. Employers post their employment opportunities and review candidate résumés for a fee. Both parties are looking for a good match, and the Internet acts as a clearinghouse to bring them together. These sites also include employment information of value to candidates, such as newsletters, salary surveys, employment trends, and related information. It's all free.

Special search engines have been developed to access job banks, and mega job banks have been created that include openings from *many* individual job banks. Perhaps the largest of these is Mega Job Search, which allows you to search more than seventy-five separate job banks simultaneously.

Each of these job banks has slightly different features. In selecting the best, choose those that have a large number of openings in their database. Their information should be updated frequently, and filled positions should be deleted. They should also have a search capability that enables you to search jobs using a number of different criteria, including skills needed, geographic location, salary level, possible relocation, and travel requirements. It's also important that the site offers jobs in your own field. If you're a nurse looking for a patient care position, you wouldn't want to search for openings in a job bank that specializes in computer technology. If you're a consultant looking for contract work, you wouldn't want to spend your time accessing job banks that cater to full-time salaried employees.

Company websites are another excellent way to learn about job openings. Many of these websites post openings and let you apply for these opportunities online. Just click on *careers* or *jobs* or *employment*. Once you find an opening of interest, you can research that company through its website or a search engine.

A word about *newsgroups*. Newsgroups have been compared to those bulletin boards you see outside local supermarkets. Anyone can post anything at no charge, and anyone else can read these postings. There are thousands of newsgroups on the Internet, and many are devoted to job searches. Job openings are posted, and interested parties send their résumés. Newsgroups, however, are *not* the best vehicle to use when looking for a job. Since there are few rules and no one is in charge of maintaining these sites, the information presented can be inaccurate and misleading. Any information you contribute about yourself can be reposted to other newsgroups to the point where you've relinquished all control.

In fact, *anything* you put on the Internet can come back to haunt you. *Any* written communication with your name on it can pop up when someone uses a search engine, and that someone might be your current boss or your prospective employer. You might make a regrettable remark on a social chat room that has nothing to do with your profession and run the risk of your boss seeing your comments. Be discreet. Never put anything on the Web that bears your name unless you feel comfortable showing it to your spouse or to anyone you fear.

As you review job openings on the Internet—or even in the newspaper—remember one thing: job ads can lie. Many job ads don't refer to a real job vacancy at all! Welcome to the real world.

Some job ads are unintelligible and meaningless. The person preparing the ad is either rushed or confused or hasn't thought out exactly what type of skills he wants for the position. Don't ignore these ads. Respond to them and ask for clarification.

Some job ads are intentionally misleading. Their purpose is to bait and switch you into another position or identify you as someone seeking employment. Ads like this are designed to draw the largest response possible. Glamour jobs in media and fashion industries are often featured, as are "lucrative" positions in management, marketing, and human resources. Respond if you like, but be aware of their intent.

Some job ads are for positions that have already been filled. The company has already found the successful candidate. This candidate might be one of its own employees seeking a different position or an outside candidate who came to their attention through a positive referral. An offer might even have been made and accepted. Why run an ad? To show upper management that every effort has been made to find the best person for the job. Answer these ads. You might impress the company and be kept on file for future opportunities.

Some ads are clear and legitimate, but you might come to those companies' attention at the tail end of the process. By the time they see your résumé, they have probably gone through all of their application files, posted the job on many bulletin boards, and offered "bounties" to other employees for referrals. Your chances of getting hired are reduced. Answer these ads as well; you might impress them sufficiently to beat the odds. If not, your name may come to mind when another opportunity arises.

Some ads are for jobs that don't even exist. These ads are often placed by recruiters who are on the constant lookout for candidates with specific types of skills. Answer these ads, too. They might not have a job for you now, but there might be something in the future. (This is another reason not to include the names of references when you give a recruiter your résumé. He might ignore your résumé and recruit your references instead!)

It's often hard to know which job announcements are valid. Here are a few warning signs to alert you to ones that may be just luring you for some other reason.

- The wording of the job announcement is vague.
- No company name is given.
- Contact information is limited to an e-mail address (no phone number, fax number, or address).
- Reference is made to "thousands of available opportunities."
- A promise of great potential wealth is made.

You lose nothing by responding to *any* job announcement, even the dubious ones, but you should be able to distinguish between what is real and what is not.

RESPONDING TO OPPORTUNITIES

Once you've found a job opening of interest, through a job bank, company website, or some other site, you can respond to this opening online. You can put your résumé, accompanied by a cover letter, directly into your e-mail message.

The rules of résumé preparation are basically the same as those outlined in Chapter I, whether that résumé is sent via e-mail, fax, or the post office. Résumés should be clean, brief, and to the point, with appropriate headings and margins.

E-résumés are rapidly replacing paper ones. In a recent survey, 34 percent of human resources professionals preferred to get résumés via e-mail, and this number is expected to increase in the future. Many job announcements, even those found in newspapers, give only an e-mail address. They don't tell you the company name, location, phone number, or fax number, making it impossible for you to contact them any way but online. Sending a paper résumé through the mail can also leave a bad initial impression, the implication being that you're behind the times and not technologically up to speed. This can be especially hazardous for older applicants.

The electronic age has also added a new dimension to résumé preparation in the form of the scannable resume. Scanning is a growing trend, especially for large companies and job banks that handle massive numbers of résumés. It will affect the words and the format used in presenting yourself and your qualifications.

Scannable résumés are designed to let employers input résumés into an electronic database and then "scan" them for specific words or phrases that indicate the extent to which the applicant does (or does not) meet the qualifications for the job in question. Scannable résumés are read by a computer, not a person. The computer has been instructed to find certain key words that the hiring authority has deemed most appropriate for a given position. You may be highly qualified for a particular job, but if your résumé doesn't include these key words, the computer will toss it out. You won't even be considered.

Preparing a scannable résumé is a special challenge. In presenting your skills and abilities, you have to be sure to use those key words that are most likely to illicit a positive response from the computer. Key words are generally nouns rather than verbs. They identify your experience in terms of categories related to skills, achievements, areas of expertise, prestigious schools, etc. For example, key words for a human resources position might be *benefits experience, BA degree, recruiting, sourcing, salary administration*, etc. Key words for a strategic planner might be *mission statements, feasibility studies, competitive analysis, goal identification*, etc.

Think carefully about these words. Make certain they describe your qualifications for a particular position clearly. Repeating the same words used in the ad or job description is one way of assuring a match. Using some industry buzzwords is another. For more help in choosing the key words most appropriate for your profession, see the *Occupational Handbook* and the *Dictionary of Occupational Titles* published by the Department of Labor and found in most libraries. Also see resumix.com. A scannable résumé should also be free of decorative accoutrements . . . no graphics or underlining or fancy borders that can confuse the computer.

Résumé job banks make it possible for candidates to do more

than respond to the job opportunities listed. They also let you put your résumé online without reference to a specific opening, the so-called *untargeted résumés.*

Many people flood the Internet with their résumés, sending them to all of the major data banks and then eagerly anticipating a deluge of phone calls with great job offers. *This will never happen.* There are already an excessive number of résumés on the Internet, and yours will get lost in this maze. *Limit your untargeted résumés to three or four carefully chosen job banks.* Recruiters are especially reluctant to follow up on résumés they receive that have no connection to a particular job search. They often get hundreds of untargeted résumés through their e-mail. If they see the same résumé come up again and again on a variety of job banks, they conclude that the candidate is either unfocused or is having trouble finding a job. Here's another tip: Don't apply for too many job openings listed on a company's website. This too smacks of desperation and a lack of focus.

The best recruiters rarely find their candidates on the Internet. This is true for two reasons.

First, recruiting services are expensive. Companies pay recruiters from 20 to 30 percent of the candidate's first year's salary. Since recruiters are generally used to fill positions in the upper salary range, these fees can become substantial. If your résumé is on the Internet, companies don't need recruiters because they can find you on their own and eliminate the middleman. Most large companies now have full-time employees whose only job is to surf the Internet for potential employees.

Second, companies use recruiters only when they can't find qualified applicants on their own. This means they're looking for extraordinary candidates rather than average candidates, and you rarely find extraordinary candidates all over the Internet looking for a job! They already *have* a job and are probably being wooed by their employer's competitors. This is why recruiters try to raid companies when looking for candidates. You don't try to find recruiters, they try to find *you* through referrals, references, cold calls, and a variety of techniques designed to uncover qualified candidates. Their target is the *passive candidate,* i.e., someone who has a good job and is not on the market but would be open to exceptional opportunities. You rarely find this type of candidate on the Internet.

THE DISADVANTAGES OF THE INTERNET

The many advantages associated with the use of the Internet in your job search are evident. Less evident are the disadvantages.

Consider the question of privacy. How widely do you want your résumé distributed? Do you really want *everyone* to see your résumé when you post it on the Internet? Are you willing to run the risk of your current boss learning that you're in the market for another position? Probably not. To avoid this, you have to know the differences between three types of résumé banks.

If you send your resume to an *open résumé bank,* anyone connected to the Internet can look at your résumé, including your current employer. Never use this type of résumé bank unless you're unemployed or have informed your present employer that you're looking for another position. In a *password-controlled résumé bank,* employers need a password before they can access your résumé. Only legitimate employers and recruiters can use this site, so you know you're dealing with reputable companies, but it doesn't protect you from the possibility that your current boss might see your résumé there and react accordingly. *Private résumé banks* are best because they give you the option of deciding, on a case-by-case basis, whether or not you want to release your résumé. Use this type of résumé bank if you're employed and don't want your employer to know that you're looking for another job. You should also use private résumé banks if you're a *passive candidate.*

Don't use the computer in your current office to respond to job opportunities via e-mail. A recent survey by the American Management Association found that 45 percent of the responding companies monitor their employees' communications on a regular basis, including e-mail, phone usage, and computer files. Forget about suing your company for this intrusion on your privacy—it's perfectly legal as long as your employer tells you it's being done.

Don't attribute this concern over privacy to paranoia. Employees have been confronted by irate employers after their bosses discovered their résumé on some résumé bank. Companies periodically search the Internet to see if any of their employees have posted their résumés there. Employers ask employees who find the résumé of another employee on the Internet to inform them immediately. People can lose their jobs or be seriously compromised as the result of such indiscretions.

Another problem with the Internet is information overload, which can produce extreme frustration. It is difficult to fathom the vast amount of information that is available on the Web. Even the most astute use of search engines can't always prevent you from getting lost in this maze of data. It's also easy to become diverted by unimportant pieces of information while losing sight of the data you really need. Links are a valuable addition to websites, but you can become so involved in exploring these links that you lose your way and have a hard time finding your way back to the original website.

Be cautious about the validity of information found on the Internet. Not all of the information presented is valid. There is no independent official body checking on the validity of this information, so you must proceed with caution.

Still another danger to be avoided is excessive use of the Internet to the exclusion of the human interaction that is so essential to a successful job search. Don't use the Internet as a crutch to avoid direct networking, which can be highly intimidating. The same is true of e-mail usage. E-mail is an efficient and effective means of communication, but it's no substitute for human interaction. Excessive use of either produces a sense of isolation and diminishes the ability to interact with others face-to-face.

Here are a few tips to help you avoid pitfalls:

- When using the Internet for your job search, remember to keep focused. Don't let yourself become distracted or confused by information extraneous to your immediate objective.
- If you find a good website with pertinent information, bookmark it so you can easily access it again. All you have to do is click on the site's bookmark and you open the site.
- If you become totally lost because you've followed certain links down a circuitous path, keep clicking on the "back" button. It will eventually get you back to the original website.
- When you access websites and newsgroups, be discriminating. Look at the credentials of the individual or organization providing the information and judge them accordingly.

- Finally, limit the amount of time you spend on the Internet to from 10 to 20 percent of the total time you devote to your job search. Use the rest of your time to concentrate on renewing old contacts and making new ones.

Advances in electronic and digital communications have provided jobseekers with valuable tools to expand and refine their search. However, they can never replace more traditional methods used in finding the best job, and they will never be a substitute for person-to-person contacts, as 80 percent of all jobs are still filled this way.

RECOMMENDED WEBSITES

There are thousands of websites out there, with new ones constantly being added and others suddenly disappearing. Given the vast number and fluid nature of site development, it's impossible to give you a foolproof list of recommended active sites. The following list should give you a start.

JOB OR RÉSUMÉ BANKS

America's Job Bank	(ajv.dni.us)
Ask Jeeves	(askjeeves.com)
Go	(go.com)
Go To	(goto.com)
Hot Bot	(hotbot.com)
Lycos	(lycos.com)
Monster	(monster.com)
Northern Light	(northernlight.com)

GOVERNMENT SITES

About	(about.com)
Federal Jobs Digest	(jobsfed.com)
Federal World Information Network	(fed.gov)
Internet Source Jobs	(statejobs.com)

Jobs in Government	(jobsingovernment.com)
Local Government Jobs Network	(governmentjob.net)
One Stop Service Nationwide	(ttrc.doleta.gov/onestop)
State and Local Jobs	(p.per/state/states.html)
USA Jobs	(usajobs.opm.gov)

ASSOCIATION SITES

Associations	(ntu.edu.sg/html/ctng/assoc.htm)
Internet Public Library List of Associations	(ipl.org/ref/AON)
Virtual Community of Associations	(vcanet.org)
Yahoo Professional Organizations	(yahoo.com/economy/ organizations/professional)

SITES FOR NEW GRADUATES

Best Jobs USA	(bestjobsusa.com)
College Central Network	(collegecentral.com)
College Grad Job Hunter	(collegegradjobhunter.com)
Internships	(internships.com)
Job Direct	(jobdirect.com)
Job Trak	(jobtrak.com)

POPULATION, JOB MARKET, SALARY, RELOCATION SITES

About	(jobsearch.about.com/library/ blsalary.htm)
Bureau of Labor Statistics	(bls.gov)
Career Path	(careerpath.com)
Census Bureau	(censusbureau.gov)
City Search	(citysearch.com)

Excite	(excite.com/travel)
Homefair	(homefair.com)
Job Resources by US Regions	(http://cdc.stuaff.duke.edu/stalum/ employment.jobresources /jregion.html)
Job Star	(jobstar.com)
Job Star	(jobsmart.org/tools/career/ spec-car.htm)
Mapquest	(mapquest.com)
Money	(http://money.cnn.com)
O'Net	(onet.com)
USA City	(usacity.com)
Wet Feet	(wetfeet.com)

RECRUITER SITES

Recruiters Network	(recruitersnetwork.com)
Recruiters on Line	(ipa.com)
Riley Guide Directory of Recruiting Firms	(rileyguide.com)

CHAPTER XI

The Experience Express Card: How to Leave Home with It

"How do you get experience if you don't have experience?"

That question is heard by more human resources, consultants than any other. It is also the most tragic statement of all because it reflects the negativism that afflicts so many people seeking employment. The tragedy is that it is based upon the false premise that you don't *have* experience. In fact, *everyone* who is the same age has the same amount of experience. It's just that some people have more in certain areas than others. The correct question is: "How do you get experience you can put on a résumé or application, and how can you use this experience in an interview?" Now you're talking!

Most people would agree that the practice of law or medicine requires a high degree of knowledge and skill. However, a practicing lawyer or doctor spends less than 10 percent of his professional time on anything that requires independent judgment. Even in these technical professions, over 90 percent of what lawyers and doctors do is based on common sense and general knowledge. The less skilled the occupation, the smaller the amount of independent judgment required. That is why automation continues to displace millions of people every year.

The saying "He doesn't have ten years' experience; he has one year's experience ten times" is far closer to reality. All that matters is acquiring the maximum 10 percent knowledge that makes one job different from another. It is this phenomenon that causes a subordinate to fear a promotion to the boss's job. Once it occurs, the bends subsides quickly. It is nothing more than an optical illusion; the view is always different from the outside looking in.

For you, the message is clear: Experience *is* the best teacher . . . so good that you need only a little bit. This reality applies whether you are starting your first job or your last. At least 90 percent of what you need comes from life experience.

Here's how you get it: Pick up the Yellow Pages, turn to the occupation you would like, and start phoning. Tell whoever answers that you'd like to get some information on a particular field or occupation. The switchboard will probably route you through to somebody. More often than not, the person at the other end will want to get rid of you, but every now and then you'll get a talker or someone polite enough to hear you out. The more glamorous and competitive the job, the more likely he'll try to discourage you, especially if you're an entry-level applicant.

Typical phrases these Whiner's Club members use to close the doors to Experience Express applicants are:

"It's the most competitive field you'll ever find."

"The entry requirements are really tough."

"It's a thankless job."

"If I had to do it over, I never would have chosen it."

"I wish someone had given me the advice I'm giving you now."

There isn't a single human endeavor on the face of this earth that doesn't have a minus for every plus. There are winners and losers in every field, and the only meaningful development in a career is from the inside out. What you do is not as important as how you do it. If you do it well, satisfaction and rewards naturally follow.

Discouraging words tell you more about those who say them than about what they actually mean. I could give you a hundred examples from my life, but you just need to reflect on your own.

You should be polite but persistent. You want something to do, and the chances are over 90 percent that you can do it with absolutely no additional training and less expensively than it is being done now (if at all). Special training isn't always necessary, and you can pick up what information you need once you are on the job. This is the one and only time in seeking employment when you should not be afraid to beg. Be flexible in your hours and earning requirements, but look for situations where duties will be varied.

Using this totally unprofessional approach may actually get you hired over the phone! You'll probably have a number of interviews arranged before you get halfway through the alphabet in the first directory. If not, just keep on refusing to take no for an answer. Remember, *it's impossible to fall when you're on the floor!*

You should guard against the "emotional carryover" that brings the rejection of the prior phone call into the new one. In *Psycho-Cybernetics,* Dr. Maltz discusses how emotional carryover can be minimized.

> If you are using an adding machine, or an electronic computer, you must "clear" the machine of previous problems before undertaking a new one. Otherwise, parts of the old problem, or the old situation, "carry over" into the new situation, and give you a wrong answer.
>
> The exercise of retiring for a few moments into your quiet room in your mind can accomplish the same sort of "clearance" of your success mechanism, and for that reason, it is very helpful to practice it. . . .
>
> If you have just talked with an irate and irritable customer, you need a change in set before talking with a second customer. Otherwise, "emotional carry-over" from the one situation will be inappropriate in dealing with the other.[10]

You know you've been victimized by emotional carryover when you call a potential employer and start the conversation by saying something like "I didn't want your job anyway!" and hanging up the phone. But that's not going to happen if you bear in mind your goal, which is to get hired, not to get discouraged. Each call is different, and each reaction will be different.

Any experience you can parlay is what you need to qualify for your Experience Express card.

The club motto is:

EXPERIENCE IS NOT WHAT YOU'VE DONE,
IT'S WHAT YOU DO WITH WHAT YOU'VE DONE.

Leave home with the card, and you'll return with offers . . . carte blanche!

CHAPTER XII

Placement Services: The Job Intelligence Network

Our office teddy bear, F. Lee, wears a T-shirt that reads: "Human Resources Knows the Best Positions." F. Lee is never wrong.

If you are like most people, you have only a vague understanding of what private placement services really are. You should know how they work and think. This knowledge will greatly magnify your opportunities for advancement in your career.

Career advisors, guidance counselors, image consultants, résumé services, and other miscellaneous enterprises are not included. Not even honorable mention, because their ability to get you hired is limited and their fees often are not.

The activities and effectiveness of outplacement consultants, job-finding clubs, job cooperatives, institutional placement services, and public placement services vary widely, making any generalizations impossible.

Placement services can be divided into three categories: executive recruiters, employment agencies, and temporary employment services. Collectively, these form the "job intelligence network."

EXECUTIVE RECRUITERS (PROFESSIONAL/MANAGEMENT/TECHNICAL RECRUITERS, EXECUTIVE/PROFESSIONAL/MANAGEMENT/TECHNICAL SEARCH FIRMS, EXECUTIVE/PROFESSIONAL/MANAGEMENT/TECHNICAL CONSULTANTS, "HEADHUNTERS," ETC.)

Executive recruiters are paid exclusively by the employer (client). Approximately 5 percent are employer-retained, and the rest operate on a nonexclusive, contingency fee basis. The fees are generally calculated based upon a percentage of the projected annual starting salary of the applicant (candidate), usually from 20 to 30 percent.

These organizations tend to be owned by management and sales-oriented individuals from almost every industry. They thrive on the chase (identification) and kill (placement). They are quick of flight, and have a positive attitude, sensitive faculties, and a keen sense of timing.

Several of the larger national recruiting organizations are owned by major corporations, and most have developed a franchise system. Virtually all the recruiters and office managers are compensated based upon the placement fees received or "cash in." Some (particularly the human resources management refugees from industry) use big words. Most know the ropes and the rules. If you use the techniques in this book when you contact them, all will want to present you for suitable openings. Then simply use the techniques to get hired.

Recruiters are successful because they know where the action is in the employment market. They know employers from the inside, where intramural politics and morale hide. They know who has exciting products on the boards, and who is about to lose key employees. They know who promotes from within and who stifles creativity. They know who pays well and who has high turnover. They know these things for the same reason you know about the interviewer . . . they listen.

Executive recruiters tend to cluster in major cities and can be found in Yellow Pages listings under "Executive Recruiting Consultants," "Management Consultants," "Personnel Consultants," "Employment Agencies," or variations on these headings.

EMPLOYMENT AGENCIES (EMPLOYMENT SERVICES, PERSONNEL AGENCIES, PERSONNEL SERVICES, ETC.)

During the last decade, more than 95 percent of employment agencies have changed their fee policy from applicant-paid ("fee") to employer-paid ("free"). They are paid on a contingency fee basis, and their placement fees are calculated based upon a percentage of the projected monthly or annual starting salary of the applicant. As you can see, there is a substantial overlap between employment agencies and executive recruiters.

If you are considering a position below $30,000, you should be focusing on general employment agencies. These specialize in clerical, administrative, semiskilled, and trainee (entry-level) placement. Even if they are employer-paid, you will find the counselors to be among the brightest, most positive human beings around. Their placements occur more frequently, and, therefore, they do not mind interruptions and assisting applicants (in confidence, if you wish). You might be talking to the owner of the business or one of hundreds of employees.

The great strength of employment agencies is their "street sense" and flexibility in serving both applicants and employers. Some are also engaged in temporary placement, expanding the options for both parties.

If you have been avoiding employment agencies because their reputation is less than sterling, take another look. Be prepared for an interview.

Employment agencies are found in almost all regions and are in the Yellow Pages listings under "Employment Agencies," "Employment—Permanent," "Personnel Agencies," or similar headings.

TEMPORARY EMPLOYMENT SERVICES

True temporary services seek registration from applicants interested in short-term or part-time employment. This is generally for clerical or semiskilled services but can extend to technical disciplines as well. They then market their services to customers (clients) and charge a specific amount for the services performed, usually on an hourly basis. When the temporary assignments are given, they dispatch their employees, and charge based upon the time records submitted. The temporary service is responsible for all payroll deductions, and may offer additional benefits and bonuses for its employees.

A temporary assignment gives you an inside look at a company that classified ads can't. If it works out, you'll get called back. You can find out about permanent jobs before they are advertised and get a head start on the competition. It's a great opportunity to make some friends within the company for that invaluable internal referral as well. Most temporary services offer a "temp to perm conversion" to customers so they can hire you directly after a certain period of time. This "try before you buy" policy is one of the best reasons to use a temporary agency, for both an employer and you.

Should you wish temporary employment, the Yellow Pages heading is generally "Temporary Personnel," "Personnel— Temporary," "Temporary Employment," "Employment— Temporary," "Engineering Services," "Computer Services," etc.

To summarize, executive recruiters open doors you thought were walls, employment agencies open doors you can't open yourself, and temporary services get you inside a company for a short look around. And for all of them, the interview is crucial.

They all know the rule: IF YOU DON'T MAKE IT HAPPEN, IT WON'T.

CHAPTER XIII
Looking While You're Still Employed: Isn't Everybody?

Ongoing job market research is fun and gives you a low-risk, commonsense way to evaluate your present position. It also arms you with facts that can be used either to negotiate more effectively with your present employer or to move more quickly if you must leave.

From the new employer's standpoint, you're more attractive if someone else thinks you're worth the salary. You communicate confidently because you're financially and emotionally more secure. These are important differences and can be used to turn any job into a springboard.

All you really need for your little do-it-yourself launching pad is high-quality personal letterhead stationery, an updated résumé, access to a computer, and a telephone answering machine.

Let's consider how to maximize your effectiveness:

1. SCHEDULE YOUR PART-TIME JOB OF LOOKING.

Looking for a job really is a full-time job. But you can't sacrifice what you have for what you want.

It's easy to become an "interviewaholic" once you start thinking about your reasons for leaving. This can distract you from your primary task of earning a living and alert your employer to your clandestine activities. You must also guard against *unconsciously* conveying your plans to your boss and coworkers. It can be a real roller coaster downhill, so be *extremely* careful in your scheduling. Do it after working hours, and use your home phone as your contact number. Secretaries, receptionists, and mailroom clerks are usually the first to notice the symptoms (cryptic phone calls, multiple "doctor visits," "Personal and Confidential" envelopes, etc.); you also may smile a lot.

Your approach to phone conversations and interviews should be that you are being paid to do a job, and it would be improper for you to take company time for personal business. Besides, you have a lot of responsibilities to your present employer, and want to be considered as effective as possible.

You get the picture: Use your integrity and stature as a basis for special treatment in employment interview scheduling. You'll get it, too. Why? Because you're just a little hard to get.

2. MAXIMIZE YOUR PERSONAL CONTACTS.

These include former supervisors, coworkers, and friends. Their assistance should be sought in two ways:

Notifying you about opportunities. Ask them to be your eyes and ears. They often delight in sharing inside information or leads that they learned about through personal observation. You should *gently* let them know if they are furnishing information on jobs you don't want. Be grateful for any assistance, no matter how ridiculous, or you may lose more than a resource and a reference . . . you may lose someone who really cares.

Presenting your background. Since they are your acquaintances, they will be working for you with the best intentions. Give them copies of your résumé and other background information. Delete anything you feel is too personal, but give them as much data as you can.

Personal contacts are a limited resource, since there are so few of them, and they are doing you a favor. Therefore, they should not be your only source for market research.

3. USE AN ANSWERING MACHINE FOR YOUR RESIDENCE PHONE.

Include only your home phone number on all correspondence and your résumé. Designate it as your "message number."

The résumé shouldn't identify your present employer in any way. Use descriptions like "Major Manufacturing Company,"

"Medium-Size Law Firm," "Newly Established Health Care Facility," etc.

Use an answering machine with remote capability. Return calls the same day or early the following day. The message should be recorded in your own voice, and state pleasantly:

> Hello! This is (*first name*) (*last name*). I regret that I am unable to answer your call at this time. However, if you leave your name, telephone number, and a brief message at the tone, I will return your call as soon as possible. Thank you for calling!

While machines turn some people off, your communication already indicates that a message is all that will be taken.

4. PURSUE ADVERTISEMENTS.

Sending résumés is easy, and you shouldn't be afraid to answer blind box advertisements. In my entire career, I have encountered only fifty instances of an employee's résumé being sent to his own company through a blind ad. I would estimate that in thirty of these, the employer either already knew the employee was running around the countryside or didn't care. In another fifteen, the discontent was nothing more than a communication blockage with the supervisor; the "forced communication" had a positive effect, and differences were resolved amicably. Four ended with the employee leaving voluntarily after a mutually acceptable transition period, and one was fired. That's a 2 percent chance. Why worry?

5. SELECT A CADRE OF PLACEMENT SERVICES.

In Chapter XIII the proper use of placement services was discussed in detail. They are the best source when you are employed, since they can present your qualifications in much the same way as a public relations representative does. They are discreet and have three things you don't: knowledge of the job market, contacts, and time. Working together, you can form a valuable alliance.

The only caution is that by now, you'll probably be considered an MPA (Most Placeable Applicant). If you receive this honor, they may try to "run" you. That means too many nonproductive phone calls and interviews.

Tell them. All celebrities have the same problem.

I hope you take this advice immediately, because the opportunities out there are just too hot to hold!

CHAPTER XIV

P.S. Soon You'll Be Hearing . . .

Ever since the Industrial Revolution, those responsible for employment have been seeking a professional identity. The titles have become more formidable: labor supervisor . . . employment manager . . . personnel manager . . . director of industrial relations . . . vice president, human resources development. Buzzwords have proliferated: aggregate workforce, applicant flow data, impact ratio, progression sequence, skills inventory, utilization analysis. A job saved here, a promotion there—it's what makes the world go 'round.

We'll be interviewing on the moon in our blue space suits, and might as well be running around caves in leopard skins for all the progress we've made in selecting one human being to work for another.

What does all this mean to you? Do you *really* think a change in the unemployment rate will help *you*? Will you feel differently if the cup is 89.9 percent full next month? Won't you still be one-on-one, getting down to business with some human being you've never met before?

Having said that, finding a good job can be especially trying in hard economic times. When it's a buyer's market, there are more candidates than jobs, with highly qualified people out of work and readily available. Employers can choose from the best.

Your challenge is to stand out from the crowd, and a highly capable crowd at that. The advice given in this book will help you to do this by giving you that special edge that distinguishes you from all of the other candidates.

The techniques in this book work. Not because I want them to, not because they're needed, but because they're based on trial and error, the same way Edison developed the lightbulb. The explanations and theories are nice, if that's your bag, but they came later. Too much analysis leads to paralysis. Break out of those self-imposed shackles and do it!

Soon you'll be hearing those immortal words: *"You're hired!"*

Oh, just in case you missed something . . . *GOOD LUCK!*

NOTES

1. Michael Korda, *Power! How to Get It, How to Use It* (New York: Ballantine Books, 1975).

2. Maxwell Maltz, *Psycho-Cybernetics* (New York: Pocket Books, 1969).

3. John T. Molloy, *Dress for Success* (New York: Warner Books, 1975).

4. Leonard Zunin with Natalie Zunin, *Contact: The First Four Minutes* (New York: Ballantine Books, 1973).

5. Maltz, *Psycho-Cybernetics.*

6. Korda, *Power.*

7. Denis E. Waitley, *The Psychology of Winning* (New York: Berkley Books, 1992).

8. Ibid.

9. Robert J. Ringer, *Winning Through Intimidation* (New York: Fawcett Crest Books, 1993).

10. Maltz, *Psycho-Cybernetics.*

BIBLIOGRAPHY . . . AND WHY

I could have written this without quoting from any other books. However, I wanted to introduce you to some references that will develop your practical skills and perceptions as you move through your career. Several years ago, the great motivational speaker Charles "Tremendous" Jones told me, "You will be the same in five years as you are today except for the people you meet and the books you read." He was absolutely right.

The stockpile of self-help books continues to grow, with most of the additions nothing more than "smoke bombs." A flashy cover, a sexy title, an inflated claim, a self-proclaimed expert. You have no time for that nonsense; you should be assessing, restructuring, and developing the techniques that will supercharge your career. I have done your research for you, and with two exceptions they are all available in paperback. Far from being smoke bombs, they are unadulterated dynamite! Not all of the titles are new. I've included a few classics because they're the foundation of all that's followed, the easiest to read, and the easiest to adapt. They're incredible, indelible, and indispensable. Buy them, read them, listen to them, and save them as part of the survival kit you will need as you continue your journey along the road of life.

Initially you should read *Winning Through Intimidation*. You might note that Robert Ringer and I write in somewhat the same style and share the same philosophy. He is a no-nonsense, get-down-to-business author, with the savvy and writing ability to back it up. (Another recommended by Ringer is *Looking Out for #1*, but read *Winning* now since we are attempting to maximize your perception when your time is limited.)

The next book that is must reading is *Power! How to Get It, How to Use It*. It is a well researched and generally accurate book. So much of the hiring matrix is ruled by silent idols. Understand them, and you can use them to your advantage. (Korda has written an excellent sequel entitled *Success!,* but you can wait.)

Another book you should read is *John T. Molloy's New Dress for Success* or its companion, *New Women's Dress for Success. Dress for Success* contains basic truths, and selective reading can get you through the book in less than an hour. Underline and act upon the advice.

I also recommend *The Psychology of Winning,* by Denis Waitley. It derives its value from the simple, eclectic, warm style of its author. It is not "must" reading, but it is suggested because it contains basic truths.

The next book I would recommend is *Psycho-Cybernetics,* by Maxwell Maltz. You will feel as though you are sitting on the lap of Methuselah, as he gives you the synthesis of 969 years on earth. The book has spawned an entire industry and is written in the same human style.

You might also wish to review *What Color Is Your Parachute?,* by Richard Bolles. It is a delightful, witty anthology that surveys the employment field. I recommend it highly as an overview but have found a more focused approach gets you hired.

These are the books I recommend. May they work the wonders for you that they have for countless others.

Bolles, Richard N. *What Color Is Your Parachute?: A Practical Manual for Job Hunters and Career-Changers.* Rev. ed. Berkeley, Calif.: Ten Speed Press, 2003.

Korda, Michael. *Power! How to Get It, How to Use It.* New York: Ballantine Books, 1975.

Maltz, Maxwell. *The New Psycho-Cybernetics: The Original Science of Self-Improvement and Success That Has Changed the Lives of 30 Million People.* Edited by Dan S. Kennedy. Paramus, N.J.: Prentice Hall Press, 2002.

————. *Psycho-Cybernetics.* New York: Pocket Books, 1969.

Molloy, John T. *Dress for Success.* New York: Warner Books, 1975.

————. *John T. Molloy's New Dress for Success.* New York: Warner Books, 1988.

————. *New Women's Dress for Success.* New York: Warner Books, 1996.

Ringer, Robert J. *Looking Out for #1*. New York: Fawcett Crest Books, 1993.

———. *Winning Through Intimidation*. New York: Fawcett Crest Books, 1993.

Waitley, Denis E. *The Psychology of Winning*. New York: Berkley Books, 1992.

Zunin, Leonard, with Natalie Zunin. *Contact: The First Four Minutes*. New York: Ballantine Books, 1975.

INDEX